In *When Music Happens*, Paul Lauzon offers us an extraordinary personal, philosophical, and scholarly experience of the poetry of music—to which he gives the name, melopoetics.

Rooted in his extensive life experience as a music therapist, musician/performer, poet, and educator, Lauzon, in Part One, weaves images of music throughout his title poem, "When Music Happens." In the reference section to the poem, Lauzon shares extensive notes on key phrases in the poem, embellishing them with a vast and truly impressive extended background of information. In Part Two, Lauzon consolidates his work with the concise but comprehensive essay, "Anatomy of a Musical Being: A Music Systems Theory of Music Therapy."

When Music Happens is a must read for musicians, music therapists, neuroscientists, and anyone who wishes to be inspired, educated, transformed by the full mind/body/spirit experience of Paul Lauzon's gift of poetry and scholarship.

Elizabeth Moffitt MTA MA
Faculty Emeritus of Music Therapy,
Capilano University

Paul Lauzon's richly layered and soul-felt poetry brings music into every fiber of our being. We walk with him in tune with the songs of the earth and the feelings of humankind while absorbing his profound research into the physiology of music making and appreciation.

Wendy Dathan, Curator of the Grand Manan Museum (retired) Author of *The Reindeer Botanist: Alf Erling Porshild, 1901-1977*

Paul Lauzon's poetry opens heart-paths to gardens of delight, stirs wave-depths of forgotten emotions, flings wide gates to unexplored spiritual realms. It is a delight to revisit again and again.

Suzanne Schuurman, educator and knitwear artist Author of *Tristan: Physically and Mentally Handicapped ... Socially and Spiritually Gifted* and *Legacy of Courage: The Life of Ola Pawlowska.*

When Music Happens

When Music Happens

Paul Lauzon

Chapel Street Editions

Appreciation of Place

Chapel Street Editions exists within the unceded and unsurrendered territories of the Wolastoqiyik, Mi'kmaq, and Peskotomuhkati people. The work we do is born from the stories carried by this land and its inhabitants. The animals, plants, soil, water, and air make this place home for the Indigenous people who belong to this land, for the descendants of those who took this land and made it a belonging, and for those who have since come from away. Chapel Street Editions holds a deep appreciation for our place within this land and the stories it tells. We honour the land's Indigenous caretakers and are grateful for their wisdom and guidance.

Published by
Chapel Street Editions
150 Chapel Street
Woodstock, NB E0J 1H4
www.chapelstreeteditions.com
chapelstreeteditions@gmail.com

ISBN: 978-1-988299-57-0

Library and Archives Canada Cataloguing in Publication

Title: When music happens / Paul Lauzon.
Names: Lauzon, Paul, 1947- author
Description: Includes poems. | Includes bibliographical references.
Identifiers: Canadiana 20250170035 | ISBN 9781988299570 (softcover)
Subjects: LCSH: Music therapy. | LCSH: Music—Philosophy and aesthetics.
Classification: LCC ML3920 .L39 2025 | DDC 615.8/5154—dc23

Book design by Brendan Helmuth

Photograph on the cover: Nautilus shell. Photo credit: Tracey Nicholls
Creative Commons Attribution 3.0 Unported license. Attribution: CSIRO
https://commons.wikimedia.org/wiki/File:CSIRO_ScienceImage_2933_Nautilus_shell.jpg

Dedication

To Manu, Ivan, Robin, Mia
for all the music you bring.

Table of Contents

Preface

Like a drop of ink stirred into a bowl of water is music in my life, your life — and yes, *music matters*. I come to this assurance initially as someone born of a mother and into a family that loves to sing. From early days I have written poems and songs that, for me, serve to make sense of the drama of existence. As a young adult I was able to travel and share my songs in performances, recordings, and musical plays. One spring day, in a bookshop in London, I found a music therapy book that changed my life. Since then, I have been a student and practitioner of this wonderful profession, gaining in experience and observation. I am grateful for the opportunity to develop my capacity for learning as teacher in a music therapy program.

Drawing upon my lived experience in music as songwriter, music therapist, and academic, I have written this *suite of poems* to evoke epiphanies of music in her many phenomenal dimensions. As *prosody* is the music of words, I offer *When Music Happens* as a *melopoetics*, a poetry of music. In part, the poems carry forward the argument presented in the accompanying explanatory essay, "Anatomy of a Musical Being." The verses go beyond the essay, interspersing data and insights from other sources including acoustics, psychoacoustics, anthropology, philosophy, spirituality, psychology, musicology, world literature, and the realm of imagery and metaphor. The "Notes" provide links to the essay and offer references to pertinent topics and publications.

My profound hope is this interlude of poetry, along with the notes and reflective essay will enrich your personal recollections, your ongoing meaningful musical connections, and encourage discovery in the wider world of music.

Part One

When Music Happens

i.

sound surrounds and shapes us

we the walkers along a shore
where song of wave
sculpts our inner earshell
the one two rhythm of walking
the one two three of breath
you turn to the cry of herring gull
her pulse, your pulse
relentless the force
of two emergent to three
the wave, the wind, the sky
notation of claw on sand

sound waves gather and travel
down the tune attuned chamber
tumbling, drumming
tympanic membrane
sensitive as an atom of gold

within the paleo chamber
middle ear chiselled of bone
released by eustachian tube
ossicles unite
hammer, anvil, stirrup

born to amplify vibration
within the skull
a sense only you can feel

passage now
through sacred oval window
to the inner chamber
cochlea
where filigree fibres
as passengers waiting to catch
the basilar train of membrane frequencies
perform transform
mechanical to electrical alchemy

in electron splitting speed
signal path firing synapses
lightning along afferent pathways
into neuro caverns of the brain
sweet kissing cousin
to the ear

ii.

origins

in the beginning was the *Word*
primal *Logos*
voicing cosmic frequencies
subsonic oscillations
beyond the animal ear
deep as first epiphany of galaxy
in endless space through timeless time

planets congeal of dust and gases
particles magnetizing ever
boneshaping mountain ridges
from darkness of boundless sky
falls blue water, oceanic H_2O
sunflares dancing aeons

the gill awaits the tidepool

to turn and turn again in
tonosphere stratosphere
atmosphere geosphere
biosphere noosphere

seasons of eternal return

with apologies to Darwin
we leap ahead by millions
of emergent probabilities
to hear Neanderthals singing
to the crested moon
Hmmmmm
the chanted musilanguage
in the vaulted cave

while in the garden
one human finds his lover
he of the brazen voice
she of the languorous lilt

is this song of songs
where music begins?
or is it moan of wind in tree?
or voices echoing across the valley
to greet the bride
in procession with her people?
or comes music with the trickster
as he mimics pebble-mouthed raven
cooing dove or screeching owl?

or is she born mother lullay of lullaby
rocking patting stroking grooming her child
in motherese of pre-natal recognition
the babbling rumbling joy of first light

the voice her very own
her chromosomes?

or comes music in the glow of faces
crackling 'round communal fire?

to share the joy of love's celebration
to excite the quested initiation
to gather forces in a hunter's cry
to chant the deities of our choosing
to raise the anchor with our shanty
to plant in rhythm of our hoeing
dance rafters loose in our raving

to swim in an ocean of air

to fulfill this longing for belonging
in the dark night of our whistling
in the soughing of cedar and pine
in frisson of the unknown sigh

all down the pilgrim road I hear them

songmakers
sooth sayers
heartbreakers
prison bar shakers
morning wakers

image bakers
crumbling wall quakers
pains takers
never forsakers
combining refining
words and tune entwining
mining the inner core

to score on clay
to wind the molten string
to bore the fingered holes in bone of bird
to shape the lyre of willow wood
to stretch the skin of antelope
to blow the river reed
to call up hope
within the hallowed tree

to let the voice
to set my people free!

iii.

quest in question

if *music*
is my question
how is *human* the answer?

she skips along unsighted
down a green corridor
into a chamber of instruments
I join this music child musicking
swaying in her body
ear to hand to foot to blinded eye
she'd been left all alone in a room
for six long years
with nothing but a radio

now she is free at last
in her twisting pigtailed beauty
to dance to the rhythm of the floorboards
to crawl her fingers along the keys
to share sweet songs of loneliness

tell me
if *human* is my question
how is *music* the answer?

the unseen one replies
in echoes of the ancient muse

stay *with* me
as in my immediate grasp
I reach out beyond
horizon of impressions
to engender understandings
of what one hears
when sound surrounds

stay we gather all
to shape our play
through kaleidoscope
of perspective
a concave mirror
a coloured mosaic
a madrigal mural
in fresco captured
to tell the tale of

where go I
on this journey of life?
with music I am
responsive
giving voice
and changing

and of what am I?
as in music composed
of nerve and sinew
feelings
stuff of mind

and what of this
primal reach to each
and every other?
with music as bridge
to nature in her fullness
to all other human animal selves
and to the great ineffable known unknown?

listen! come the bells

come the bright solstice bells

on ribboning wave!

iv.

I respond

like the complex turning
of gears within gears
conjoined to one another
in the finest Swiss
self-winding watch
my ticking brain
engages more than
a hundred periodicities

some longer than a day
the seasonal mensural cycles
infradian rhythms
of planet and her moon

we add some once a day
circadian rhythms
as messenger molecules
release melatonin at midnight
into pineal gland
and sweetly thicken blood
to greet the lark
at rose-coloured dawn

we live the arc
of sun across horizon
and unto dusk
when pause she gives
for sleeping

and within my dreaming stir
and flow ultradian rhythms
rapid eye movement to deepest sleep,
and this my basic cycle
continues in my waking
when beyond the ninety minutes of my purpose
I must lower the beta
to alpha frequencies
or pay the price
drain adrenals
coax the migraines
call forth the ambushing chaotic
hobgoblin symptoms
of bodymind and mood

comes the music
I tap my foot to binding beat
sing come walking down the street
entrain vibration to sympathy
yours and mine

sway in the frame of the shaman drum
leap to the chime of twelve string kithara

as she strums

join hands to the pulse
and to patterns of pace
migrations to the fertile crescent
a dance across the steppes
to the drum of hunter's snare
a droning of the pipes
an arrow whizzing past my ear

I hear the bardic voices as they pitch
inside the storm of epic song
all prosody and phrase and timbre
I move to these, the storied melodies

Love sings in our communion time
the spondees trochees
and iambs of every day

while the chorus of believers
gather me in their wake
and I would break if not
for their holding of me myself

in their consonance coupled
to tribal mythologies
in morphic undertones
of algorithmic overtones

dissonance, you have my attention!

v.

giving voice

this deepest impulse
to be heard
the need for belonging
to mean something to someone
to pick myself up
a hundred times a day
as fall I must
in learning to walk to live
to listen and be listened to

I hear the voice of others
long before I hear my own
from deep in deepest well
reverberations
voices re-sounding

I am born into a language
ancestral residue of reaching out
each to each

in this language a music
a polyphony of breath
vowel consonant alphabet
diphthong and syllable
as words emerge

from out the wrenching cry
of primal need and want
and babble I with you
who hold me close and closer
to whisper in my ear

as humans each
we have our instrument
a voice!

you know me so well
perhaps you do not hear me?
my inner speech is hidden
behind my eyes
yet I hear myself when I sing

and your reply in counterpoint
a witness, a presence
in my thoughts
now spoken from yours
to my inner voice
as you reach from inner
to outer speech

from this dance of waves
this endless duet
the song is born
I am born!

vi.

changeling

she calls me to herself
to the beating of her heart
to the twenty-nine turnings in her sleep
to the swirling cadences in her breathing
to the dance of river blood in her veins
long before the eye will see
through walls of darkness
my ears ease to hear her voice
her own my very own mama

at the now of my birth
a flash of firsts
to brighten the clearing
vast spaces of wind and water
of sunlight streaming through the leaves
this murmur of sunlight
a lullaby of freedom
shush ... linger at the breast
let mother do the rest
baked bedecked in my glowing skin
throbbing in my skull
as twitch the limbs
I sit I crawl I roll I stand
I walk I run I dance

I answer to my name is me
and I am the sound
that answers to yes and no
to do and don't
scratching letters into fences
tracing signposts onto walls
and floating sticks
in ditches a boy can revel in

and river washes over me
again again
this river of becoming
a radiant boy who haunts
the library in the fields
the running lad
whose legs can leap
and o'erleap into somersault
of hands and elbows, arms and knees
as swing the limbs of change

songs become the markers
of my days
bubbling as from a rock
on forest trail
each a wave that breaks
unto my awareness
an undertow of overtone
the pelting summer hail of song

words born not to forget
how we choose our own regrets

we coast the love well met
in the steam of evenings
gathering as only the young can gather
andante life a dream
slow liquid shining
undulating love a presence

holding onto silence
I have wrapped her in my arms
and she a fledgling
flown into the night
gone once given

sorrow woe as sorrow wells
and spells like scars remain
raining raining raining

step by step you trace
the fathomed highway
the unmarked trail
assert the one you keep becoming
as strings resound beneath the fingered nail
your arms embrace the quivering
spruce and rosewood
the bronze vibrating
laughter of strings

and I a changing self
am music changing

see! the snow that falls from heaven
melts before my eyes
to water running into streams
that one cold and freezing night
becomes translucent sheet of ice
whence love can walk on water

this music makes the
coneflowers, the hyacinths, to grow!

vii.

song of bodybrain

I hang from a branch
on morning tree
stretching shoulders arms and spine
toe to tip the rooted grass
let go the weakening grip
as I fall to gravity of being
my full weight upon the ground

pulsations of temple
as signals at speed of sound
travel down auditory canal
as signals at speed of light
travel upwards spinal column
through to stem
and shake the cerebellum
fear and flight
freeze and fawn enfolded
into reptilian brain

journeying on
to pre-mammalian middle brain:
do you remember hippocampus
how you yearned for amygdala?
and Virgil hypothalamus
how you led Dante pituitary

through realms of appetite
and beyond?

or how in your nurture days
you grew the bark of cortex
on mammalian spreading tree
the brambling branching billions
of nerve endings, each a beginning
to create the great frontier
within your skull?

geography of lobe and cortex
frontal parietal occipital
sensory motoric auditory visual
continents of being
oceans of expanse

see how walnut-shaped in hemispheres!

your left brain
chants her mastery of sequence
crisscrossing corpus callosum
and on to right brain
as she connects
in her ontological synchronicity
a dance of wonder
a mystery deep as solitude
at the moment of creation

and shift you shift both night and day
a creature swaying
metabolic in immunity
in dominance and clutch of stress
shaking the leaves
as you digress from beta
through to alpha and omega

while the pioneers of now
the sharp-tooled explorers
hope to find the slippery *mind*
within your folds
their digits digitizing notions
still coming up ones and zeros

a bridge to cross the creek undoubtedly
will not span an ocean

and still you carry on
in feathered lightness
as consciousness expands
and circles in the warming winds
uplifting diving into slipstream
divining clouds of unknowing
in every when and where
underpinning weathered intuition

the stuff of which we are made
as music is the art of air!

viii.

homage to feelings

we hide nothing we show all
your every look a self portrait
to grace the garden wall

witness the rose
she has her leanings
in reflecting sun and moon
shivered by the honeydance
of waggling bee come noon
while oak tree casts a shadow
the trout leaps in her pool
and quietly the cat
she strokes my foot
with whiskers
all nature blisters
in the rub of feelings

I show my face
in survival dress
drives of thirst and loneliness
call me to bed and board
to praise the Lord
as I come up for air

prepare to meet
emotions I have felt
and will surely feel again
fear and rage
curiosity love and shame
sadness and joy unbounded

being who I am

these motions
come most unexpectedly
in waves upon me
involving I
and Thou revolving
shaping from the inside out
this need to sigh
to shout

elemental
in my sanguine tempers
continuum of choleric
on to melancholic
or dyed in the wool
phlegmatic
of moods that linger
much like the weather
on days I struggle

to find the words the letters
the natural colours
soothing threads
a sheltering hat

and what of that,
of music and tears you ask?
what happens when I hear
your sad and lonely song of love?
does it make me sad
or shockingly am I happy?

am I the loved one in the song
or the lover who sings?
or am I the song?
is this what listening brings?
or could I be some poet
far enough away to view the battlefield
from glistening tower across the river plain?

and when I sing for sorrow
will she bring all my tomorrows
back again?

like you, passing through
I am emotion, a notion, a thought
performed in pleasure or in pain

surely love on laurel wreath will bring
heart filled with passion lost
in tears that fall like rain
catharsis leaves me empty
full salt sting of wisdom found
within refrain

sing with me now my love!
come sing with me again!

ix.

webs of meaning

a girl can do it
can hear a music in the words
and whistle walking
rhythm a stick upon a fence
she sings her freedom
cliff diver turning in air
because the leap is there

a flame can do it
can bring family 'round
communal fire
laughter food and warmth
later the deepening awe
the catching gasp
at raven's song of creation
a memory of smoke and stars

and in my own my lyric time
images dreams
and sweet anticipation
of one mystical chestnut tree
sounding re-sounding
resonance of consciousness sustains
as one low D sharp string
I pluck it now

for a melody can do it
and you my love are falling awake
as chorus sings the slow air
and dancers from over mountain
lock into swing of jig and reel

music sounds as feelings feel . . .

he watched as she left home
as she journeyed from out the *one*
to find her shadow self
way out beyond the *five*
eager bound to hear the totem prayer
and at the *twelve* her turnaround

hitchhiking home prodigal repentant
with one treasured amethyst in her satchel
one insight joining all

that time is the now
of being changing

and music is her language
note to note engaging
spreading webs of meaning
ineffable in intention

rounded tone to interval
to motif to phrasing
lowering and raising
bringing forth another voice
a sister theme extending
blending into fugue
that has no ending
crescendo diminuendo
diversion conversion
contrary motion opposition
plagal cadence to contrition
a turmoil bound for peace
of tension and release

an ear can do it
can gather threads
of ringing strings
and make them real as feelings
and this is what I meant
when I offered but still
could not find the syllables
lost within the words
until I heard the cooing dove
and so, I sang your name
O Nameless One
a sound to break the darkness
in thunderbolt of light

a hand can do it
can hold steady the point of pen on paper
coax outflowing words from within the ink

I found you at the brink
composing and arranging
music ever in the now
as time is the now of being changing!

x.

earthsong

rain awakens the sun
patterns pulsing
falling onto leaf
who sighs for breath

Gaia opens her soul
softens her soil
to rivers in the running groove
of this gentle rain
which from dusk to dawn has fallen

Gaia rhythms me
in a ululating flow of waves
random continuous
hypnotic to the barefoot one
who leaves her print
upon the dappled sand
who in turn receives and holds
the weight of all anxieties

ebb and flow of tide inexorable
will wash away
these footprints and your thoughts
moon and tide
will grind these stones

to a trillion trillion grains of sand
bones of your driftwood identity
strewn upon the beach
for spirit to reach
and take hold of

and oh! the cold the bite
of hollow fog borne winds
dark clouds drifting
over teal beach grasses
the twisted near-uprooted
scrags amid the rocks
above the shore

despair not!
for sun breaks through on this
the every morning of the world
fanning golden across your eyes
to joy your heart
to still your mind

five four
three two one
slow your breathing 'neath the sun
become in this moment
the graceful deer who turns
her head her capturing ear
to symphony of morning

the orchestra is tuning

whistling quail, bickering hen
splashing mallard, pitying dove
a whir of tiny insect wings
blue jay shouts her cry of love
nesting plea of fleet sandpiper
thrum of bullfrog in the reeds
crackling leap of paw on twigs
hammering beak on knotted bark
the wind through velvet pine

I hear dolphins singing
to the moon hovering still
in morning sky
while humpback gathers
from deep of dream
to leap to breech
above the ocean
laughing

out of one silence
as day is long
in diverse voices
we laud you!
we praise you Gaia
in our song!

xi.

variations on my relations

a bringing back
restoring narration
life lived fully in relation
and music is my bridge

sister, if I do not sing
my voice still will echo
the rasp of songs on fragrant nights

brother, if I forgo
swordplay of guitar
my fingers yet shall weave
you a coloured sash for dancing

mother, if I do not cry
my eyes as violets
reflections of the love you gave
I place upon your grave

father, if I speak no words
I leave the raga winds to blow
ignite aeolian strings
to release, to guide you on to healing

and love my lover
you and I, we two as one duet
to linger in the cooling mist
that hovers in pregnant air
above the lake
a cymbal crash to break
to greet the storied sun
to drum the cardamom for tea
life poured out as love
is freely given

and daughter son
blood of my blood
teacher of my heart
my hand is ever here
to lift you and to let you go
in glow beyond all expectation
to dance this story of your life

and friend my friends
in counterpoint of engagement
you gather rhythms of our breathing
sharing songs of seasons
reverberations shaking and shaping
sand into celtic knots
on head of drum
somehow become as someone
I myself can recognize

for you my friend have loved
and cherish me now
through all my changes

cousins, generations all my kin
pages in akashic songbook
a music scored in ink of ash
intricate as lines on cheekbones
etched of winter winds
we catch a moon to carry songs
beyond the glistening trees
I know you from your voices
you join in songs of paddling
echoes in the eddied pool
accordions violins guitars
for a Sunday afternoon

these gifts instruments of music
so full of use and beautiful
in shape and texture
in natural wood and polished brass
in fabric of human fabrication
I applaud you in your measure
and in your pleasure
trace the boundaries of myself

and all living things
who swim who fly who run

who leap who sway who sing
I glory in your presence

and if I have not named you
know that each unwritten letter
each endless variation is
a tender wash across my heart!

xii.

psalm for the known unknown

the beat of ear to heart to feet
I begin to slow the wheels
notice how I feel
inside my breath a voice
emergent entrained
in altered state of mind
a dance of alpha delta waves
of transcendence am aware
internal affirmations
personal prayer

stepping into
dare I say, mystical music
of communitas woven
of melody of harmony
in chants and hymns
antiphony, the sacred dance
organ pipe to shake the nave
the choir in flight entranced
in prosody of words revealed
by Manifestation
circling round the Lote tree
beyond which lies
seventh heaven

I cannot see invisible
but I hear You
I cannot hear the soundless voicing
but I see You
a God who dances!

I listen play and sing
sudden insight of creation
music calls me to vocation
this longing to know and value
truth beauty goodness home
each moment crystallized
as music lives only in the now
this assimilating intersection
of what has come and is to come
a ripe and speckled fruit
upon the bough

new song awakens
sends contemplation out
into the world on wings
of sound of silences
untrodden ground
beyond both us and music
where dwells the known unknown
a consonance of rhythm
the bells in modulation
of our deepest yearnings

the wind that flickers candle
Shaker and Sufi in their turnings
Cistercian monk his Kyrie
Yogi in her cycling mantra
the child in peel of joy at play
the wanderer who sings the rain
beneath the tree of solitude
the walls that shake in hallelujah
as congregation shouts her freedom
the cymbals bells trumpet drum
the war torn in their cellar crying
we rattle on
we rattle on in Babylon
release us Lord, give us song!

in voices joined
will peace come to our world!

xiii.

this particular I

oh, member of the village tribe

a human becoming
as unfolding sonata
an irreducible ordered whole
greater than the sum
of all partials, tones and spaces
I am open system

self-monitoring and repairing
ever shifting into balance
of steady state homeostasis
I am melody meandering
the rising falling roadway of life
as fireworks of vitality affects
come and go continuous flow
of input output
constancy

and when challenged
by loss, distress
the anxious chaos of life
I struggle to compose

of long-lost chord
a healing modulation
exploring a circle round of fifths
organic adaptation transforming
into this new key of here
and me now

and I composed of many parts
subsystems
am whole within myself
a system
and still myself am part of larger wholes
supra-systems
family tribe society culture
all sister species of planet earth
and notice how
in structured hierarchies
great chain of being
the symphony survives
while random notes
go scattering in the wind

moving forward
in form and function
in praxis of dynamic morphology
I offer

music as sound
time-ordered in rhythm
trans-verbal in melody
performed in human play
of harmony

I name these
open natural music systems
rhythmos tonos harmonia!

xiv.

rhythmos

as earth turns
and circles round the sun
all is vibration periodicity
oscillation
rhythmos a sequence
of recurring patterns in flow
the swing of pendulum perpetual
begun more than four point five
billion years ago

diurnal nocturnal
through dusk and dawn
circadian clocks in rod and cone
from eye to pineal gland of sparrow
you marvel at how bees in flight
time their floral rendezvous
to sun arcing across the sky
and in mammals all
the dance of everyday
in suprachiasmatic nuclei

inner conductor beats and keeps
ensemble of human body
all organs linked

to a coalescing collective tempo
as drumbeat of the mother's heart
gives promise of purpose wholeness
and you the answering pulse

rhythmos sympathetic
cosmic endogenous
in hormone and hunger
in mind and feeling
brain wave and pain wave
in breath and heart and sleep
ordered wholeness of great
complexity and reach

rhythmos open to environment
speeding up and slowing down
in cadence tempo time and pulse
measure throb swing and stress
in balance of endeavour
in common time of walking
in three four time of breath
a bio-musical homeostasis

rhythmos a force for change
in the face of challenge
generating new and personal
signatures of time duration and pace

a welcoming hand upon the dance floor
a smile of synchronicity
a celebration of grace

rhythmos from primal come and go
on to pulse and gathering cycles
of three to six to twelve eight time
in growing polyrhythmic fractals
to become long lasting
slowly running waves of structure
as chambers of the heart
in schemes of recurrence
flowing like rivers in oceans
are able to support the quick
and easy beat of enriching blood
from vein to artery
in humans and in galaxy

as seasons come and go
we are born of rhythmic flow
moved as music moves
to the beat of all creation!

xv.

tonos

it begins with an inbreath
diaphragm lowering
lungs filling expanding
stomach torso chest
I hold the warming breath
and with intention of expression
raise the diaphragm
this my *generator*
sending air across the vocal folds
vibrator larynx to hold
in time and tension
as if in miracle a tone
emerges *Hmmm*

I lower jaw open mouth
let sound reflect on palate
and upwards into sonic caverns
resonators in my skull
moving on to greet *articulators*
teeth tongue and lips
shaping vocal-ease
speech held and energized
into song to reach altered state
of mind emotion

tonos I, a sound making
creature, complete in voice
and ear to auditory cortex
I sing I hear can tune
my voice and modulate expression
as vox vibrates my body
penetrates awareness
complete in polyphony
of self to self and other
an echolocation in life

tonos in my phrasing
contours melody
enacts a narrative of resonance
simultaneity repetition
trajectory of character
and breath supports this voice
locked into rise and fall
and rise again
connects the wandering feelings
finds a balance

tonos changes
deepens in her breathing
resets the drone of natural pitch
to one in resonance of emergent persona
as she expands her repertoire
of basic human calls
laughing sobbing sighing
groaning screaming crying

she vocalizes to make things
right with the world
as outer voice reflects
the inner being

tonos in each fundamental sound
of breath releasing
the *Ahhh* flowers into vibratory
rainbow of overtones
original frequency cloned
higher and taking you higher
invariant law of nature
alive in every tone
combining into binary
and every rounded form
of music the language

we join the tribal narrative
in patterns of expression
in communal interaction
each of us our own instrument
tonos the voice

generation re-generation
comes the glee girl
comes the song man
I sing, therefore I am!

xvi.

harmonia

we take one string, one nerve
the length a wilful walking pace
and stretch our silver chord
between two rosewood blocks
on resonant chest of spruce
the monochord of Aristides
and there discover
in crystal pool of number
that as one becomes many
the many become one

divide this single string
exactly at the centre
pluck and hear how
she doubles into octave *doh doh*
in rising harmonics, in overtones
we unlock the key for tuning
ratio of 3 over 2
doh sol a perfect fifth
ratio of 4 over 3
doh fah a perfect fourth

string mind ear
finger touch of string vibration
conjoined to rational mind
with resonance of tone in ear
string heart ear
we live in changing tonalities
major full of strength and contrast
minor free of mutual inhibitions
play we play in music
building ladders
to scale the barricades
of heaven

harmonia a gathering
a vertical stacking of tones
in one simultaneous moment

harmonia a horizontal counterpoint
of interwoven melodic motifs
resonant in all living organisms
expanding our sense of consonance
of concord, a sounding together
we find new tolerances of dissonance
of discord, the pulling apart
and scrambling on to unity

we seek and find harmonia
smiling in her many faces

cosmic as in Kepler entranced to the measured
    music of orbiting heavenly bodies

in flora fauna and animals finding balance
    of foothcld in the wildness of habitat

in humans gathering to find agreement
    negotiating in rituals of living

in your quest for healing correspondence
    of feeling thinking doing of bodymindsoul

in *harmonia* of self-identity, your song attuned
    to inner rhythms of consciousness

in beauty, sensation of aesthetic proportions
    sounds movements coloured things

in sub-sonic tone of devotee, one voice singing
    a full chord in overtones of enlightenment

in gathered truth of stories teachings laws
    of polarity confluence coherence

in proportion of numbers and geometric shapes
    golden section of growing leaf and nautilus

in that what can be, ought to be, fulfillment
of the good in unity of possibilities

in *harmonia* I include
the liberties of discord
here to shake perfection
from her boredom
as freshness and zest arise
from intensity of individuality

you have a role to play
in your gathered raiment
unwritten script
the audience settles
we darken the background
you step into foreground
into spotlight on the stage

and sing the words
of heart and soul's deep stirring
as you engage in harmonia of being!

xvii.

therapeiā

first, do no harm!

you find the voice of sad of joy
fear love shame of burning mad
all emotions wedded into song
ancient tempered *imitation*
as feelings crescendo in music
a sweet release, a letting go

catharsis outpours, restores
and you walk on

or is music a bridge
for building trust in give and take
of counter and transference
in confidence of listening deeply
of insight born in waiting
in rubato of attention
relationship a journey
upon a sea of restoration
sails on drumming waves
to greet the coming squalls
in anchored breath
co-therapist of song

and still more deep-rooted
are we not made as music is made
and so potentially can be healed?
as in meadow field of *rhythmos*
we sway to cycles of nature in her turning
dawn to noon to dusk and to dark night
as in *tonos* voiced in feeling melody
of twists and turns, in passages of song
or gathering as in harvest cycle of *harmonia*
patience planning cultivation
growing into habits of illumination
absorbing, ever learning to play ...

we open another door, my friend
stories of persons I have known
come boiling in my mind

Laura centrifugal turns her head, her gaze
    as smiling mother rings a chiming lullaby

Darren travels, round and round he comes
    to mallet and to gong here in our circle

Billy leaps from chair, force of twelve string guitar chord
    played upon life's pier, her ship comes in

Carl sings, his stream of consciousness simmering
    a poetry of joy in adolescent angst

Tyrone returns from weeping church, finds a beat,
    raps you-got-me rhymes for grandfather's passing

Tanya on the ward, back from the brink, raises the stick
    then drives her anger through a frame drum

Mark attends to gently down the stream and merrily finds
    his once lonesome self, inside a round of voices

Francis dials down the wheel of head-on collision pain
    as she wanders winding beach in her mind

Georgie in print dress and stuttering tears, says
    please play that song again, it makes me cry

Joseph lost in miles of hallways, numbered doors
    why don't they come see me anymore?

Charles in palliative, as sons and daughters gather round
    sings of glory, grace, and steamboat ride to school

Belva of twisted limbs, glows from her daybed
    in vision of herself as the lucky loving one
    she is my teacher

    and I, of the walking wounded

    therapeíā, do tell
    I hear lilacs in your voice
    have surrendered to your spell!

xviii.

silences

if I could be a silent one
then surely, I would hear

silent moon as she sends her threads
of light for deep diving whale to weave

silent sky shaping silhouette
of maple trees bleeding sap to sweetness

silent friend who lingers unseen
a third one here in our deepest conversation

silent rooted cliff face watching patiently
waiting to send voices back in echo

if I could be a silent one
then surely, I would hear

silent tears, as I pass and catch you crying
hiding in a hallway of loss alone

silent changing season of snow
thawing into crocus violet and daffodil

silent dawn and trees in aspiration
towards the sky as silent night falls to earth

silent wind who softly enters after storm
of thunder and crashing wave, a stillness

if I could be a silent one
then surely, I would hear

silent one who first must hear *courage,*
her own something to say before she speaks

silent one in solitude who knows
of blessed mercy and speaks gratitude in his heart

silent speech of lovers, a joy in communion
of two persons, to love and to be loved

silent anticipation at the coming birth
of each new name, a new language

if I could be a silent one
then surely, I would hear

silent dream begins to sound in music
a gentle unity of far and near, for you to hear

silent pause between two sounded tones, two beats
a measure of truth, of electric brain and beauty

silent spaces growing more intense
and loudest as the music dies away

silent gestures in your story, intimations
of possibility as I get to know your shadow

if I could be a silent one
then surely, I would hear

once silent realms
now full of sound and noise
come whispering as
I learn to listen further

I hear silence as the sound of time passing

and inlaid into silence
this poem
mozaic of words
a contemplation of music

I leave a silence in every
syllable for you
to speak your poetry
of heart and tone

at home in the wide
reverberant milky dome
where, when music begins
fullness happens again
and hush again!

Part Two

Anatomy of a Musical Being

A Music Systems Theory
of Music Therapy

Prelude

I have engaged in many meaningful musical moments, and from the first have been deeply compelled to ask, *why is music effective in life, as therapy?* To get to the bottom of this question I realized I first must consider music more broadly by asking, *what happens when music happens?* To answer this global question, I then developed the notion of *music state*, meaning the way music basically *is* in the human organism at a given time. Since music and human are conjoined, I linked this topic of "when music happens" to three important questions for every human life: *where go I?*, *what am I?*, and *what of the other?*

To answer *where go I?*, essay section 1.3 presents music states that are 1) responsive, 2) expressive, and 3) changing, which correspond to poems iv. "I respond," v. "giving voice," and vi. "changeling."

To answer *what am I?*, essay section 1.3 presents music states that are 4) neuro-biological, 5) emotive, and 6) cognitive, which correspond to poems vii. "song of bodybrain," viii. "homage to feelings," and ix. "webs of meaning."

To answer *what of the other?*, essay section 1.3 presents music states that are 7) ecological, 8) relational, and 9) transpersonal, which correspond to poems x. "earthsong," ix. "variations on my relations," and xii. "psalm for the known unknown."

My next step was to consider that *music states* are experienced by a *musical being*—a music child growing into musical adulthood. To understand a musical experience from the *inside out,* within a musical context, I was led to consider that we are wired for sound, that a *musical being* has *musical systems.* To speak of systems required a deep dive into natural systems theory.

There are four major features for all natural systems: 1) holistic, 2) self-maintaining, 3) responsive to change, and 4) coordinating. I asked if *musical systems* have these features and can thus be considered systems in the strong sense. I argue that they do, and they are. My further intuition was that we should give these musical systems each a name, whereby we could develop a method for practice, research, and thinking concerning *natural musical systems.* To speak of rhythm, melody, and harmony in a more humanly activated manner, I have chosen the (Greek rooted) words *rhythmos, tonos,* and *harmonia.* These terms refer to musical events, qualities, and capacities within the human being—*the musical systems of a musical being.*

Abstract: The goal of this essay is to work towards an answer to the question, "Why is music effective as therapy"? The general features of the music state, as experienced in therapy, are outlined. Through a step-by-step process, features common to all natural systems are integrated into a music-centred answer to the question of effectiveness by outlining a new contribution to music therapy discourse—Music Systems Theory.

1   Introduction

1.1   The Question

Music. The word conjures, it evokes, it rings, it baffles. We know what it is, and yet we don't. For some, it is nothing but a background rumbling. For others, at the opposite end of the continuum, it is a deep mystery to be explored.

As a music therapist, I strive to understand music with clarity and depth. Otherwise, how can I know what I am doing when engaged with the other and still be true to myself as a musician and therapist?

For some time in the modern history of the Music Therapy profession, the goal has been to answer the pragmatic question, "is music effective as therapy"? This advocacy has been necessary to establish the profession of music therapy in the modern health care world. Everyday, in her work, the music therapist answers this question — in her treatment planning, in her achievement of therapeutic outcomes, in her extended body of published research. Also, we see the profession growing internationally; it would most likely not be so if music were not effective therapeutically.

We come to the more difficult question. We ask, "*why* is music effective as therapy"? We move beyond recognizing the phenomenon of music as effective to attempt an understanding of *why* this is so. My purpose in this essay is to respond to this question of effectiveness in an authentic and comprehensive manner, one that will contribute to the ongoing dialogue in the community of engagement that is music therapy.

With this purpose in mind, it is helpful to mention that Aigen (2005, pp. 23–28) differentiates between three approaches to theorizing about music therapy: 1) *recontextualized theory* explains with concepts from other disciplines, 2) *bridging theory* uses terms from other disciplines in combination with those specific to music therapy, and 3) *indigenous theory* is original and specific to music therapy. For Aigen and others, a theory specific to music therapy would be "music-centered." My work has also been informed by other examples of those working to develop understanding concerning the therapeutic effectiveness of music: Aldridge (1996), Bonny (2002), Bruscia (1987, 1998a), Eagle (1996), Kenny (2006), Nordoff and Robbins (2007), Pavlicevic (1997), Priestley (1994), Rider (1997), Ruud (1998), Smeijsters (2005), Stige (2002).

I believe that if one imposes a theoretical construct from another field of study onto music therapy, whether it is behaviourism or psychoanalysis, for example (See Ruud, 1978), then one is essentially working from the "outside in." I agree with Herbert Read that, "If you are translating form in one material into form in another material, you must create that form from the inside outwards" (Read 1931, p. 255). We are, after all, using words to describe another medium, music. The words we use need to resonate with the authentic experience of music therapy.

1.2 Definition of Music

To help determine the scope for the following inquiry, I present this working definition: *Music is sound as time-ordered, trans-verbal play. Sound* is what is heard. *Time* is the "indefinite continued progress of existence and events in the past, present, and future regarded as a whole" (Oxford, 1996)). *Ordered* is methodical arrangement. *Trans* is the going beyond, the travelling to the other side of *verbal*, the language of words. *Play* is free action, considered as active spontaneity, rather than reactivity (Winnicott 2005).

This definition of music is meant to allow a broad conception of music, one that includes manifest sounds from three identifiable musical realms: 1) the music of culture (made by humans), 2) the music of nature (emanating from the natural world), and 3) the music of self (the music of the individual). For example, one may consider the different rhythmic characteristics of each: 1) the rhythm of nature is *flow*, continuous yet random, 2) the rhythm of culture is *groove*, a periodicity that is measured and coordinated among the players, and 3) the rhythm of self is literally *pulse*, personal and purposefully moving to maintain the steady state in both psyche and soma. These rhythmic attributes of music are all *time-ordered*, but in different ways, and so are included in this definition of music: *sound as time-ordered trans-verbal play*.

1.3 Music States

My path of inquiry is to follow the "impulse to reduce to clarity and thereby get a systematic and comprehensive hold" (Honderich 2001, p. 16) on the nature of music, specifically as it affects the human reality. My underlying conviction is that the more we understand music, the more clearly we fathom what it is to be human, and vice versa. This conviction is based on a broader premise that, "Like conditions give rise to like results throughout the cosmos: this is the basic credo of our natural sciences" (Laszlo 1996, p. 59).

This path involves the process of *correlation* (Tillich, 1967, I, pp. 59–61). What I am *putting together in relation* is music and humankind. I am not interpreting them as polar opposites, but rather as generating a mutual interdependence, both essentially (in possibility) and existentially (in actuality). For example, if *human* is the question, then how is *music* the answer? Conversely, if *music* is the question, then how is *human* the answer? Perhaps more clearly, I am moved by another person making music and I want to know, *What happens to her, to me, when music happens?*

This question about what is happening is one about correlating *music* and *human*. To do this I bring forward the concept of "music state." By this notion I mean the way music basically *is* in the human organism at a given time — an occasion of now; it refers to the fundamental properties of this condition (Audi 1999, p. 876). Music state represents a clear and simple concept for linking music and humankind.

I begin by creating a profile, making a list of the most significant attributes of music states in the context of music therapy; generally, a theory of music therapy "which makes sense of these features is to be preferred to a theory which does not" (Ravenscroft, p. 2). (Elements of the following discourse borrow structure from Ian Ravenscroft's excellent "Introduction" in *Philosophy of Mind, 2005*).

The present question is, *what happens when music happens?* The answer I propose is contained in this list of nine fundamental properties of music states one experiences through music: 1) responsive, 2) expressive, 3) changing, 4) neurological, 5) emotional, 6) cognitive, 7) ecological, 8) relational, and 9) transpersonal.

(Note: In the following narrative, "Jones" and "Smith" represent someone engaged in music therapy, either as therapist or client, *or* Jones and Smith may also represent people more generally engaged in music outside of music therapy. Both interpretations are possible.)

1. Responsive

Some music states are caused by states of the cultural environment.
For example, Jones responds to a rhythm he hears by tapping his foot. This means that the music state is open to influence from the outside. Whether he realizes it or not, Jones is receptive to the musical stimuli coming from the music and sounds of the cultural environment — the voices, instruments, and technology, alone or in combination. His organism is open to rhythm, melody, harmony, timbre, dynamic, and musical form. Music states are responsive.

2. Expressive

Some music states cause action. Jones sings; he plays a drum. He is able to send vibration out into the environment. He expresses himself. He redirects the energy from within outward. Why he does this is not clear at the moment. He just does it. Music states are expressive.

3. Changing

Some music states are correlated to personal growth. Jones is as he is in this music state. He was different before. He will be different in the future. So, where is the real Jones? What is his identity? Is it in his body, his memory? Is he motivated to change, or is he being motivated to change? Does this change follow a natural developmental course? How is music related to this change? Jones head is spinning with these questions. He knows, we know, that music is affecting him; every tenet of music therapy states that we are to bring about a *positive change* in Jones. Does this mean supporting him as he is, or redirecting him? Who gives us permission to do this? Music states are about selves in change (Pivcevic 1990).

4. Neurological

Some kinds of music states are systematically correlated with certain kinds of brain states. Recent advances in neuroscience show that music is a global phenomenon in the brain (Hodges 1996; Taylor 1997; Rider 1997; Levitin 2006; Schneck and Berger 2006; Sachs

2007; Patel 2008). We know that various areas of Jones' brain are stimulated by sound, music, movement, memory, emotion. There is nothing going on with Jones that is not firing somewhere in his brain. But there remains what has been called the *explanatory gap* between brain states and phenomenal experiences, between the objective and the subjective. This is another way of saying the mind/body split is still not resolved. In other words, "It's one thing to give neurological explanations of the various relationships between our [music] experiences; it's quite another to explain the [music] experiences *themselves*" (Ravenscroft 2005, p. 185).

5. Emotional

Some music states have qualitative depth. Jones feels the music. He is enraptured with the sound. His phenomenal consciousness (Block 1997) feels now joy, now pain, now boredom, something. For a time, he lost his hearing, and the quality of his music state was different, muted. His music state is steeped in emotion.

6. Cognitive

Some music states are about things in the world. Jones recalls the meaningful moments he has had with music. The music represents something to him: memory, context, image, metaphor, a symbol of longing. It stimulates his access consciousness (Block 1997). Theories of musical meaning range from referential (music refers to something non-musical) to absolutist (music has no meaning but the music itself). Jones is somewhere in the middle, an expressionist; he finds music as being like life, that "the elements of music are related to and share important qualities with basic human experience" (Wigram 2002, pp. 36-37). In this moment he experiences release of tension, conscious of his own awareness that he is experiencing the relaxation response. Jones' music state is a thinking state, a web of cognition. (See Lauzon 2006a).

7. Ecological

Some music states are caused by states of the natural world. For example, Jones is influenced by the music of nature, the wind and waves, the deeper cosmological patterns. Once he becomes attuned, this music is capable of grounding Jones in the extended manifest world around him. "Eco" is the home base; that which we need to survive. Jones considers that he must renew and maintain his connection to the natural world. He finds this connection very much alive in traditional world musics. His organism is open to the rhythm, melody, harmony, timbre, dynamic, and musical forms embedded in the natural world. Music states are ecological.

8. Relational

Some music states cause music states in the other. Jones sings and Smith responds. He is surprised that she responds like this, but she does. In this moment, they share energy, a trans-verbal understanding. This connection may lead to other connections. He has precipitated a condition where relationship may develop. Smith and Jones, Jones and Smith, together in time, each in their own musical state, yet sharing something. Music states are relational.

9. Transpersonal

Some music states expand the self into other realities. Jones asks himself the bigger questions: Why am I here? Why do bad things happen to good people? Do we live on after we die? Is there a God? What is a good life? Every time he sings the sacred music of Bach, the hymns, the chants, he feels a part of a much larger world—a world of worship and prayer and vocation and good deeds, enchantment, purpose. He finds connectivity all around him. He intimates that somehow it is beyond him, beyond anyone. Music is transpersonal.

1.4   Grouping the Music States

We now organize these nine fundamental properties of music states according to how they relate to the individual human being, who for our purposes we call the 'Self." The three dimensions relate to how the self acts in the world, how the self is structured, and how the self connects to the other.

The first three aspects (responsive, expressive, changing) we group as

THE JOURNEY OF THE SELF

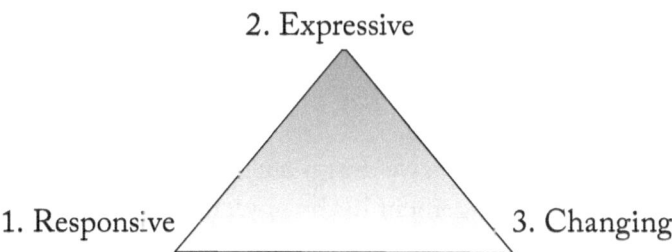

The next three (neurological, emotional, cognitive) are based on form and structure as

THE LEVELS OF THE SELF

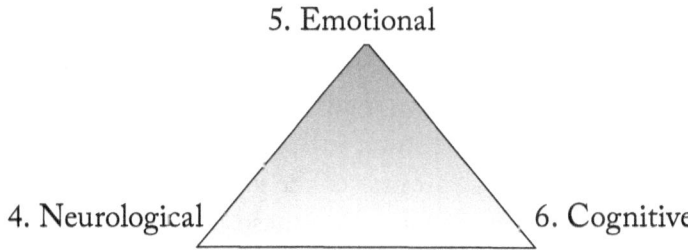

Finally, the last three (ecological, relational, transpersonal) are based on how music is the sea for the island of self to reach out as

THE SELF AND THE OTHER

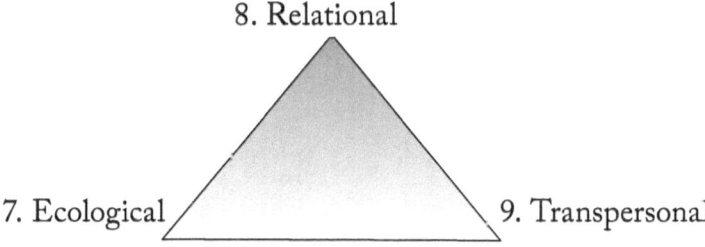

1.5 Grounding the Music States

I also suggest another layer of understanding within each of the triads. The left side of each triangle may be considered the *ground*, by which I mean the basic background morphology of the dimension: in 1, *responsive*, we have the ground for human dynamic movement; in 4, *neurological*, we witness the basic connector for the biological pattern; in 7, *ecological*, we have the natural world around us, our literal *ground*.

The top of each triangle we designate the *foreground*, the place of our most visible engagement in the now: in 2, *expressive*, we see the external self coming out of the inner self, communicating to the world; in 5, *emotional*, the self discloses the many variations within the world of feeling; in 8, *relational*, the self connects with the other.

Finally, the right side of the triangle is the *new ground*, that which emerges on a new level of experience for the self. In 3, *changing*, the self is learning through the experience of living; in 6, *cognitive*, the self uses the rational mind to integrate the body and feeling, as well as to understand the past, to be alert in the present and to plan for the future; in 9, *transpersonal*, we witness the self moving into an awareness of the vastness of being.

One way of further understanding these connections is to use the dialectic approach of thesis (ground), antithesis (foreground), and thesis (new ground).

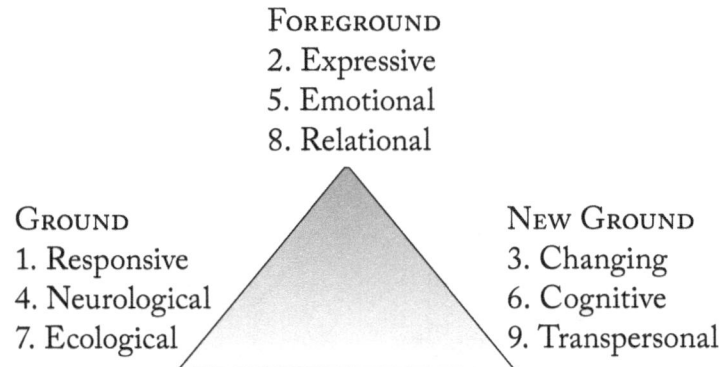

FOREGROUND
2. Expressive
5. Emotional
8. Relational

GROUND
1. Responsive
4. Neurological
7. Ecological

NEW GROUND
3. Changing
6. Cognitive
9. Transpersonal

2. Music Systems Theory

2.1 Rationale

A tourist in Paris comes upon three workers and asks what they are building.

The first replies he is laying bricks. The second says he is constructing a wall. The third, with a flourish, explains he is building a cathedral!

This story speaks to the historical (and often interpersonal) tension between analysis and synthesis. Every discipline needs a constant source of new empirical data. This information must then be categorized and analyzed. Ideally, we take the next step; a turn to synthesis not simply as speculation, but as a conjoining of various sets of seemingly unconnected information into a constructive understanding of the discipline. The specialist becomes the generalist who is able to see the big picture; you examine the tree whilst remembering it is part of the forest.

General Systems Theory (GST) is particularly helpful for creating synthesis. GST is a trans-disciplinary study of the common organizational invariances of different phenomena. In other words, in this approach one tries to see the similarities in various things and processes and to describe the underlying systems that make them work together to create larger wholes. Systems theorists see common principles in the structure and operation of systems of all kinds and sizes.

This discipline was pioneered by biologist/philosopher Ludwig von Bertalanffy (1901-1972). His goal was to develop a method that could be adapted for universal application with a common language and set of concepts. Since the early 1950s, GST has been applied to many disciplines in the sciences and humanities, including, but not exclusively, biology, psychology, economics, ecology, agriculture, social sciences, and philosophy (Davidson 1983, Skyttner 2001). I have appreciated Carolyn Kenny's use of *field theory*, a category of General Systems Theory, in her ground-breaking theoretical work in music therapy. I have also been particularly drawn to the work of GST theorist Ervin Laszlo

(1972, 1996) as well as Ludwig von Bertalanffy (1968) and will use this approach to help answer our question about the effectiveness of music as therapy.

2.2   The Musical Being

We saw how Jones had different kinds of experiences while in his "music state." Let's give Jones an integrated identity as a living breathing "musical being." This kind of language has been in use for decades in music therapy. In a passage that describes the responses of the special child to improvisational, interactive music therapy, Nordoff and Robbins write:

> The *music child* is therefore the individualized musicality inborn in every child: the term has reference to the universality of human musical sensitivity — the heritage of complex and subtle sensitivity to the ordering and relationship of tonal and rhythmic movementand to the uniquely personal significance of each child's musical responsiveness. (Nordoff and Robbins 1977, p.3)

This concept is at the core of Nordoff/Robbins work, a model of music therapy that has ongoing impact in the community of care. To imagine a *music child* inside a neurodivergent or disadvantaged child child allows the music therapist to listen, to appreciate, to engage.

Suppose the *music child* was to grow into the *music adult*; I take liberty to call this changing musical person the *musical being.* As the title to this essay states, we now move forward to outline the *anatomy of the musical being.* I approach this as an enquiry of *we are* rather than *I think.*

> I concern myself with being only in so far as I have more or less distinct consciousness of the underlying unity which ties me to other beings of whose reality I already have a preliminary notion. (Marcel 1951, p.17)

2.3   Natural Systems

Jones in his combined music states has become a musical being. I have shown how this resonates with the concept of the music child. I come to the logical next step. Taking a cue from systems theory, I now describe the *musical being* as having *music systems*. In the language of GST, a system is any entity maintained by the mutual interaction of its parts. Think now of how the early medical doctors finally began to understand the human organism when they determined that she had physiological systems — circulatory, respiratory, digestive, etc. They were able to describe the substance (morphology) of each system and its various parts, as well as the functions (physiology) of that system as a whole. For von Bertalanffy, *isomorphisms* are "structural likenesses that reflect a commonality in the way the parts of a system relate to each other" (Davidson 1983, p. 173). His notion of *dynamic morphology* is that substance and function should be treated as different approaches to the same phenomenon. For me, this is a search for *correlation* of form and function in the human and musical domains.

I am not saying that musical systems are the same as physiological systems. They are different. In fact, as we shall see, they reorganize human anatomy and physiology in attunement to music; what they share are common organizational features of all open working systems. For von Bertalanffy (1968), a system is either isolated from its environment (closed system), or continuously exchanging matter/energy with its environment (open system). As an open system, a *natural system,* is one that "does not owe its existence to conscious human planning and execution" (Laszlo 1996, p.23). GST has identified four organizational features common to natural systems: 1) ordered wholeness, 2) maintenance of steady-state, 3) self-reorganization in the face of challenge, and 4) hierarchical fit in a multi-holon reality.

> 1. *Natural systems are wholes with irreducible properties* (Laszlo 1996). A whole possesses characteristics that are not possessed by its parts singly. A natural system has the quality of ordered wholeness.

2. *Natural Systems maintain themselves in a changing environment* (Laszlo 1996). They are open systems in a steady-state. That means that they are self-monitoring and self-repairing. Constancy is maintained by a continuous flow of input and output. The precise regulative mechanisms of warm-blooded creatures that we call 'homeostasis' is an example of steady-state.

3. *Natural Systems create themselves in response to the challenge of the environment* (Laszlo 1996). When subjected to constant external forces, systems can reorganize their own constraints and acquire new dimensions in a process of *adaptive self-organization.* "The progressive transformation of organic species pushes the front of evolution forward" (Laszlo 1996, p. 60).

4. *Natural Systems are coordinating interfaces in nature's hierarchy* (Laszlo 1996). In the natural world, organisms that last do so because they are hierarchically organized. In the course of evolution, hierarchies are more efficient than non-hierarchies. A natural system is part of a "multi-holon" structure.

Holon is Arthur Koestler's term for wholes that are also part of other wholes. A holon functions as a whole on one level, and as a part of a larger whole on the higher level. Below it are its parts, called the "subsystem," and above it is the "suprasystem," of which it is a part. "An organism displays not only a morphological *hierarchy of parts* but also a physiological *hierarchy of processes*"(Von Bertalanffy 1952, p.42).

2.4   Music Systems

Apart from biological needs humans share with animals, we live in a world not of things but of symbols (Langer 1957).

One major realm of human symbol making is *discursive,* as in the communication of information and meaning in language. Music can be understood as a non-discursive, experiential symbol making system. There is a deep intuition at work here. How is it possible that I make music unless I am somehow made as music is made?

Further, what is music to us? How do we understand it? Let's go back to our definition— *sound as time-ordered trans-verbal play.* Each of the elements of this definition of music brings forward a part that is essential to the whole. In the long history of musicology, we see these same dimensions of music being brought forward for analysis and understanding: rhythm (time-ordered), melody (trans-verbal), and harmony/form (play). Granted, the notion of harmony as understood in the West is not always practiced in the same way in the music of other World Music cultures. In these musical worlds, the simultaneity of tones is expressed in polyrhythmic and polytonal group performance, a kind of horizontal rather than vertical harmony.

In concert with the above definition of music, I choose to frame the discourse concerning music systems with these three aspects of music: rhythm, melody, and harmony/form. I move the discourse forward by asserting that the *musical being* has three *music systems*: 1) *rhythmos,* 2) *tonos,* and 3) *harmonia.* I deliberately give each a name. I identify them as existing within the human organism. This systems model is presented equally as structural and functional, a *dynamic morphology.* I aim to present an organic conception, leading to an integrated view of the biological and musical properties and to the uses they have in humans.

2.4.1 Rhythmos

Rhythmos is the system that makes the individual a rhythmic being, manifest in the basic periodicities and cycles of a human life. Jones would take solace in this description of his early formative days:

> Accompanied by the powerful drumbeat of the
> mother's heart, the being is shaken to the core by

these pulsations, which promise purpose, wholeness, synchrony. Secure in this rhythm, the being's own heart takes form and begins an answering pulse. As soon after birth as possible, the mother takes the baby in her arms and puts its head against her heart. The rhythm is still there, a reliable beat against which to measure the flow of growth and change.(Leonard 1978, p. xi)

If we are to speak of *rhythmos* as a human music system, we would be well served to examine it according to the four organizational features common to all natural systems.

1. *Ordered wholeness is essential to rhythmos.* The essence of wellness in humans is an agreement of the moving parts so that the organism may work as a whole. In studying human disease physiology, we identify such elements as rhythms of pain sensitivity, activity rhythms, cosmicrhythms, endogenous rhythms, muscular rhythms, pain-wave rhythms, rhythms of blood circulation and respiration, rhythms in sleep, breath, heart, and others. (Scheck and Berger 2006, p. 142)

This brief list points to the rhythmic nature of all physiological systems and the necessity of coordination of these rhythms. There are cognitive rhythms and emotional rhythms. The emerging science of chronobiology tells of infradian, circadian, and ultradian rhythms. Neuroscience dwells in part on the frequency of our beta, alpha, delta, and theta brain wave states. Donald Hodges points out that, "Brain waves, hormonal outputs, and sleeping patterns are examples of the more than 100 complex oscillations monitored by the brain" (Hodges 1996, p.43). There are multiple manifestations of rhythm in the human organism. This broad subject is the work of many researchers and awaits a thorough meta-analysis within the musical systems theory. Suffice it to say, *rhythmos* manifests as an ordered wholeness of great complexity and reach.

2. *Rhythmos is an open system in steady-state.* Our rhythmic system is constantly adjusting itself to maintain a biomusical homeostasis. It is an open system, subject to rhythmic influence from the environment. As an example, witness the use of sedative and stimulative music to both slow down and to speed up the organism.

3. *Rhythmos has the capacity for creative self-reorganization in the face of challenge.* Rhythm is something we get better at the more we do it. Michael Thaut points out that, "auditory rhythm improves the temporal, spatial, and force aspects of the total movement pattern in therapy and not just the timing of movement endings in coincidence with a beat" (1999, p. 238). *Rhythmos* provides a flexible system of many levels, generating new patterns for the arrhythmia of our lives.

4. *Rhythmos is a coordinating interface in a hierarchical structure.* All rhythms are forms of periodicity. The rhythmic subsystem is *vibration*, that level where sounds manifest and take shape. Vibrational units join together to become the holon *rhythm*, a regularly recurring motion that proceeds in time-ordered, alternating sequence. One important element of the periodicity called rhythm is *pulse*, the ongoing, steady, underlying beat. Another aspect of rhythm is *pace,* the duration of the space between pulses. Lastly, various holon-rhythms join together in the suprasystem *cycles*, the level where larger *patterns* emerge, patterns connected to many more natural systems. The cycles of musical rhythm interface with biological rhythms to make *rhythmos*.

> *Periodicity,* the tendency of an event
> to recur in cyclic intervals, is one of
> the basic foundations upon which
> physiological function is sustained, and
> is an inherent characteristic in music.
> (Scheck and Berger 2006, p. 138).

The process manifest in human *rhythmos* is similar to that of our physiological systems, in that this process in sustained by its underlying forms, for example, as the pre-established structure of the heart supports its function of rhythmical contraction. Von Bertalanffy describes this conjoining of form and function:

> What are called structures are slow
> processes of long duration, functions
> are quick processes of short duration.
> If we say that a function such as the
> contraction of a muscle is performed by
> a structure, it means that a quick and
> short process wave is superimposed on
> a long-lasting and slowly running wave.
> (Von Bertalanffy 1952, p.42).

2.4.2 Tonos

Tonos is the music system that organizes humans as sound generating beings, particularly through the voice. Tone is a building block of melody, and being less dependent on cultural meaning than *melody*, the word *tonos* will allow for extended application in describing this music system. When Jones feels, he vocalizes. The range of sounds he makes presents a wide range of emotion. Here is a description of *tonos* when considering the four organizational features common to all natural systems.

1. *Tonos is a system with ordered wholeness.* Anatomically, the tonal system includes all of the sound generating,

sound receptive, and sound processing structures: lungs, vocal folds, resonators, articulators; the outer, middle, and inner ear, as well as complex neurological connections including the auditory cortex in the brain. These physiological features work together so Jones can vocalize; not only does he sing, he tunes his voice, he modulates his expression.

2. *Tonos maintains itself in a changing environment.* Notice how the breath literally supports the voice in keeping a steady state. Burrows observes that,

> a number of different human sounds, the voice among them, result from the stratagem of tapping into the primary activity of breathing. Sneezing, snoring, snorting interrupt the flow of air at the nose instead of the larynx; wheezing and gasping are protovocalizations, gasping exceptionally taking place on the intake (Burrows 1990, p. 29).

The tonal system integrates human melody as a symbolic expression of basic emotion:

> Along with laughter and sobbing, the limited repertoire of human calls include: groaning in disapproval; sighing as an expression of sadness and weariness, fatigue, or relief; and crying with pain, fear, and/or remorse. These six human calls and their variants are exclusively available to all human animals. Diagnoses and dysfunctions of any kind seem not to impede employment of these basic symbolic calls, except in cases of severe

damage to the amygdala...(Schneck and
Berger 2006, p. 161).

We use vocalizations to make things right with the world, both within and without.

3. *Tonos creates itself in a changing environment.* It is clear that various aspects of *tonos* can change profoundly. One changing aspect, the breath, is understood as key in all schools of mind/body wellness. Another set point for *tonos* is the individual's "natural pitch." This is one's characteristic drone note when speaking in a relaxed manner. As we change over time, so does our natural pitch adjust to the emergent persona. Also, we expand our repertoire of the above-mentioned six basic human calls. The outer voice reflects the inner being, telling the ultra-verbal story of our lives (Austin 2008).

4. *Tonos is a coordinating interface in a hierarchical reality.* The tonal system is based on vibrational frequency that we interpret as pitch. Each fundamental "ahh" that Jones expresses contains its own vibratory rainbow of "ahh's." This world of harmonics is an organizational *invariant*, one of the most dramatically beautiful in all of nature—each fundamental frequency cloning itself into higher and higher realms. This subsystem of harmonics makes the holon tone that in turn combines to make larger structures, a suprasystem of musical language. When listening to Jones, we hear the real connection between his music and his language, the connection between emotive meaning and referential meaning. The connection of music and verbal language is not merely a metaphor; they share underlying biological similarities (Patel 2008).

2.4.3 Harmonia

For the ancient Greek, the word *harmonia* meant:

> the joining or fitting of things together, even the material peg with which they were joined (Homer, Od. V. 248), ... especially the stringing of an instrument with strings of different tautness, and so a musical scale (Guthrie 1962, p. 220).

Roget gives these additional meanings for the verb *to harmonize*:

> Be harmonious, be in tune or concert, chord, accord, symphonize, synchronize, chime, blend, tune, attune, atone, sound together, sound in tune; assonate; melodize, musicalize. (Roget, 1977).

From this brief listing we see that harmony brings together all other aspects of music, particularly rhythm and melody. As we will see, the music system called *harmonia* easily takes on the four attributes common to all natural systems.

1. *Harmonia is a whole with irreducible properties.* By definition, harmony is ordered wholeness. This fitting together of parts so as to form a connected whole is strikingly similar to the concept *health*, which we describe as "a quality of wholeness associated with well-being." Musical harmony can be experienced as a vertical stacking of tones in one simultaneous moment, or as a horizontal counterpoint of interwoven melodic motifs. This unifying force has resonance in the human organism.

2. *Harmonia maintains in a changing environment.* This is an open system, constantly moving to maintain a steady state. Consider the concept *consonance*, literally a 'sounding together," and *dissonance*, a "sounding

apart." By driving the sounds apart, dissonance initiates and maintains movement. Consonance brings the sounds together by reconciling them into a structure of wholeness. "The unison is actually the only consonance, compared to which all other musical experiences are dissonances of varying strength" (Levarie and Levy 1983, p. 121). The biological mechanisms of *homeostasis*, and the more recent theory of *homeodynamism* (Rider 1997), show the play of *harmonia* in a human life.

3. *Harmonia creates in response to the challenge of the environment.* Natural systems tend to go to ordered steady states, but most states are relatively unstable. In the play of harmony we select a few tones from the many, progressively developing new steady states that are more resistant to the dissonance than the former ones.

> Our proposal regarding the relationship between music and its benefit for clinical practice rests on the proposition that our human identity is like the identity of a piece of music continually being composed in the moment (Aldridge and Aldridge 1999, p. 85).

We compose a life. We perform health. We bring together the disparate elements into an ordered whole that is new. "Self-organization radically modifies the existing structure of a system and puts into question its continuing self-identity" (Laszlo 1996, p.47). *Harmonia* is a dynamic system, helping us to deal with the inner constraints we have to forceful challenges by creating an adaptive pathway to a new identity.

4. *Harmonia is a coordinating interface in nature's hierarchy.* At the "eureka" moment of scientific discovery, in the peak moment of artistic expression, there is a sense of oneness that many call harmony. In this music system we alternate between microcosm to macrocosm. The subsystem is atomic, vibrational, the harmonic series. In the next holonic level we make harmony in music. Interestingly, the historical development of harmony in Western music coincides with the developmental structure of the harmonic series itself: unison, parallel fifths and fourths, triads, the chordal seventh, and on it goes. *Harmonia* is such that one suprasystem follows another:

> We are natural systems first, living things second, human beings third, members of a society and culture fourth, and particular individuals fifth—we can make our own classification along such lines. In any case, we know ourselves if we know how basic characteristics of organized nature are specified to issue in that *sui generis* individual which each one of us turns out to be on close acquaintance. (Laszlo 1996, p.21)

3 Answering the Question

3.1 Music States and Music Systems

Our next, and not insignificant, task is to determine if *music systems theory* provides an answer to the question, "*why* is music effective as therapy"? To accomplish this, I return to our original list of the most significant features of music states in the context of music therapy. Briefly put, we have characterized these as, 1) responsive, 2) expressive, 3) changing, 4) neurological, 5) emotional, 6) cognitive, 7) ecological, 8) relational, and

9) transpersonal. I have suggested that a theory of music therapy that makes sense of these features is to be preferred to a theory that does not. *Music Systems Theory* has been developed with this challenge in mind. I will examine each feature of music states in light of the three music systems. This process will allow for further clarification of the systems in terms of structure and function, as a dynamic morphology. What follows is a description of the properties of music states in music therapy in the *language* of music systems.

1. *Some music states are caused by states of the world.* Jones responds to a rhythm by tapping his foot because his *rhythmos* is actively entraining with the outside environment. Musical systems are open to input from the environment. This input includes all aspects of *rhythmos* (pulse, pace, pattern, etc.), *tonos* (pitch, prosody, phrase, timbre, etc.), and *harmonia* (consonance, dissonance, dynamic, form, etc.).

2. *Some music states cause action.* In terms of active engagement, *rhythmos* is the key music system. That being said, it is clear that both *rhythmos* and *tonos* have an actively expressive dimension. We can think of the two combined as a 'tonorhymic' system. Jones sings; he plays a drum. He is able to send vibration out into the environment. He expresses himself. He redirects the energy from within outward. The balance of response (#1) and expression (#2) is coordinated by *harmonia*. We recall that all music systems are open systems moving to a steady state.

3. *Some music states are correlated to personal growth.* Music systems are flexible, able to facilitate change of all kinds. Musical milestones of development can be carried on throughout a person's life. *Harmonia* provides a constant for Jones sense of his own identity.

Music systems provide a structure where he can find motivation to change from within. At times, this change is sudden, unexpected. At other times it follows a natural developmental course. In an article on therapeutic improvisation, I have shown how change can be directed within a musical model of interaction (Lauzon 2006b). In another essay, I have examined the notion of *change* in music therapy in relation to the mimetic, interpersonal, and music-centered theory groups, and have shown how change is possible in a music systems model (Lauzon 2006a). Whether the music therapist is working with the notion of *change* from a supportive or a re-directive stance in the therapeutic moment, it is my view that music systems can provide a cogent, true-to-the-work approach for clinical practice in music therapy.

4. *Some kinds of music states are systematically correlated with certain kinds of brain states.* There is no question of this; we have defined the music systems as being embedded in the human organism as a whole, including the brain. We have already mentioned that recent advances in neuroscience show that music is a global phenomenon in Jones' brain. Music systems provide one answer to the *explanatory gap* between brain states and phenomenal experiences, between the neural and mental awareness. Music systems have the capacity for both *curing* (an outer phenomenal procedure), and *healing* (the individual's inner force for wellness), because as natural systems they are open to input from outside, whilst embedded and working within the person.

5. *Some music states have quality.* As mentioned earlier, *tonos* integrates human melody as a symbolic expression of basic emotion. When Jones sings and

plays, he feels the music. He is enraptured with the sound. He responds more easily to some music because it speaks to him. This is beyond *taste* in music; it is about a deep psycho-bio-musical connection. All music systems have quality, but *tonos* is the key to emotion.

6. *Some music states are about things in the world.* Stephen Brown contends that music and language have evolved from one original "musilanguage" (Brown, 2000). In a way, *tonos* is like that original form of expression, combining both the emotive qualities of music and the meaningful capacities of language. Psychologically, music is a real experience in the now. For Jones, music is meaningful, it represents something to him, stimulates his access consciousness. In *Frames of Mind*, Gardner considers that we have a *musical intelligence:*

> As an aesthetic form, music lends itself especially well to playful exploration with other modes of intelligence and symbolization ... Yet, according to my own analysis, the core operations of music do not bear intimate connections to the core operations in other areas; and therefore, music deserves to be considered as an autonomous intellectual realm (Gardner, 1993, p. 126).

This is *harmonia* at work, stimulating access consciousness. Jones' *harmonia* is an authentic experience in the moment, helping him to make sense of things. It is a force for balance in the dimensions of his life, coordinating his *I think* with *I feel* and *I do*, for example.

7. *Some music states are caused by states of the natural world*. Jones is influenced by the music of nature, the wind and waves, the deeper cosmological patterns. As mentioned earlier, our definition of music — "sound as time-ordered trans-verbal play" — allows us to speak of three kinds of music: the music of nature, of culture, and of self. Each of these in turn can be described by their own unique adaptation of rhythmos, tonos, and harmonia. I have outlined these distinctions in the following table:

Music of	NATURE	CULTURE	SELF
RHYTHM *Rhythmos*	FLOW Random	GROOVE Structured	PULSE Personal
MELODY *Tonos*	SOUND Cosmos	SONG Group	VOICE Solo
HARMONY *Harmonia*	LISTENER Essence	ACTOR Presence	INSTRUMENT Resonance

8. *Some music states cause other music states*. Jones sings and Smith responds. He need not be surprised that she responds like this, his *tonos* is engaged with Smith's *tonos*, as is his *rhythmos*. This time-ordered, trans-verbal understanding may lead to deeper communication. He has precipitated a condition where relationship may develop. One excellent description of music at work in a therapeutic relationship is Carolyn Kenny's *The Field of Play* (Kenny, 1989/2006). Her work creates a model of *harmonia* in client/therapist engagement.

9. *Some music states expand the self into other realities*. Jones realizes that although he is not exactly the centre of the universe, he can at times perceive the larger web that connects him to sacred, ineffable realities. The meditative, spiritual journeys of the world's religions and their mystical approaches have

a rhythm, a song, and a harmonious intent that goes to the core of living this passage here on earth. The lightning strike of insight, the thunder of realization engage Jones and Smith, lifting the quotidian life to greater meaning. These realizations have found expression in the history of ideas from Plato's eternal forms, through Renaissance notions of the "great chain of being," to the modern quasi-mystical language of quantum physics, and most recently to the advanced approaches of systems thinking and the ecological worldview. We are all, each of us, part of a grander rhythm, adding our individual song to the endless chorus of creation.

In the foregoing I have tried to demonstrate how the *Music Systems Theory* of music therapy makes sense of the phenomena of music states by providing a music-centred language to describe the core operations of a dynamic natural system.

4 Further Considerations

4.1 Summary

In this essay I have suggested the question, "why is music effective as therapy"? is an important theoretical consideration. In answering the preliminary question, "what happens when music happens"?, I made a list of features common to *music states*. I said a theory that makes sense of these features is to be preferred to a theory that does not. I insisted that Jones not only has music states, but that he is a *musical being*. I then determined that the musical being must have *music systems*. I articulated the four organizational features common to all *natural systems*. I described our three music systems, *rhythmos, tonos, harmonia* as natural systems with the four common features of natural systems, 1) ordered wholeness, 2) maintenance of steady-state, 3) self-reorganization in the face of challenge, and 4) hierarchical fit in a multi-holon reality. Lastly, I gave answer to our original question of effectiveness by making sense of the features of music states with *Music Systems Theory*. This theory is able to provide explanatory language for all of these features: 1) responsive, 2) expressive, 3) changing, 4) neurological, 5) emotional, 6) cognitive, 7) ecological, 8) relational, and 9) transpersonal.

4.2 Conclusions

There are several good reasons why the working music therapist should consider *Music Systems Theory* as a sound framework for understanding and explaining her work.

1. This is a *music-centred* theory of music therapy. It is a *bridging theory* that uses terms from General System Theory in combination with those specific to music therapy. It is an *indigenous theory* in that it creates new theoretical concepts (rhythmos, tonos, harmonia) with the intent to explain the work from the inside outwards.

2. While building on previous knowledge of musical structure, this approach gives her a *new vocabulary* for her work, one that is specific to music therapy.

3. The theory takes a general, synthesizing approach, respectful of both science and art. This allows for integration of all emerging *research* in the field. It builds on the ongoing *music states* contributions of all those who study natural systems.

4. The method used in this inquiry—examining the features of *music state*—can be used as a common language to be shared with other theoretical approaches to music therapy. Also, the whole notion of *music systems* is intended to be generative of new realizations that often emerge through dialogue.

5. This theory has adaptability. A person entering into the study of music or music therapy may grasp the basic notion of music systems, while, at the other end of the continuum, music systems can be examined in depth and specificity by researchers, scholars, and experienced practitioners from a variety of related disciplines.

It is clear to many in the field of music therapy that a new and emerging paradigm for music therapy theory is germinating in the notion "music-centred." *Music Systems Theory* is offered as a step along that path.

"Why is music effective as therapy"? I reply that we are made as music is made, with *music systems*. To be effective, the music therapist works with these music systems.

Why is Music Effective as Therapy?

Music States	Music Systems	Natural Systems
(What happens when Music happens)	*(The Musical Being has Music Systems)*	*(Four features of all Open Systems)*
1. Responsive	• *Rhythmos*	1. *Ordered Wholeness*
2. Expressive	• *Tonos*	2. *Maintenance of Steady State*
3. Changing	• *Harmonia*	
4. Neurological		3. *Self–Reorganization*
5. Emotional		
6. Cognitive		4. *Hierarchical Fit*
7. Ecological		
8. Relational		
9. Transpersonal		

Glossary for Part Two

Closed system. A system considered to be isolated from its environment.

Correlation. Mutual relationship of interdependence of two or more things.

Dynamic Morphology. The view that morphology (form) and physiology (function) should be treated as different approaches to the same phenomena.

General Systems Theory (GST). A holistic way of thinking based on an awareness of the behavior of systems in general. The proposed discipline that would seek and apply general systems laws.

Harmonia. The music system which brings together all aspects of the musical being in ordered wholeness.

Health. A quality of wholeness associated with well-being.

Holons. Systems in hierarchical order. Wholes that are also parts of other wholes.

Homeostasis. The living organism's process of self-regulation, as in the regulation of body temperature.

Isomorphisms. Structural likenesses that reflect a commonality in the way the parts of a system relate to each other.

Morphology. The study of living forms.

Music. Sound as time-ordered, trans-verbal play. (Lauzon).

Musical Being. The individualized musicality inborn in every person. (Adapted from Nordoff/Robbins).

Music state. The way music basically *is* in the human organism at a given time; it refers to the fundamental properties of this condition.

Music system. A musical dimension maintained by the interaction of its parts in the human organism.

Natural system. An open system that does not owe its existence to conscious human planning and execution.

Open system. A system that continuously exchanges matter/energy with its environment. Includes all systems that are alive.

Periodicity. The tendency of an event to recur in cyclic intervals.

Rhythmos. The music system which makes the individual a rhythmic being, manifest in the basic periodicities and cycles of a human life.

Steady state. A basic characteristic of open systems, in which constancy is maintained by a continuous flow of input and output.

System. Any entity maintained by the mutual interaction of its parts.

Tonos. The music system which organizes humans as sound generating beings, particularly through the voice.

(Aspects of this Glossary are adapted from Davidson 1983, pp. 223-228)

Notes for Part One

i. the sound surrounds and shapes us (p.2)

sculpts our inner earshell: Murray Campbell and Clive Greated, *Musicians' Guide to Acoustics*, p. 39-67; Siegmund Levarie and Ernst Levy, *Tone: A Study in Musical Acoustics,* p. 163-167. The acoustically informed reader will notice that in this account I follow the *signal path* of sound vibration.

of walking ... of breath: Siegmund Levarie and Ernst Levy, *Musical Morphology*. Levarie and Levy point to the ambiguity and tension happening when the metric 2 (heartbeat, walking) is coupled with the organic and rhythmic 3 (inhalation and exhalation)—for example, as experienced in syncopation (Greek *syncope*, "cutting into pieces"). p. 243-248.

cochlea: the snail-shell-shaped, fluid filled spiral structure of the inner ear, where sound vibrations are converted into electrical impulses that the brain interprets as individual sound frequencies.

ii. origins (p.4)

in the beginning: John (Gospel) 1:1 *The New Jerusalem Bible*. In the Old Testament the Word or Wisdom of God is present with God before the world existed.

noosphere: Pierre Teilhard de Chardin, *The Phenomenon of Man*. Teilhard argues that the *Noosphere* (Greek *nous*, mind or intellect) develops through *noogenesis*, "the engendering and subsequent development of the mind." p. 181.

Hmmmmm: Steven Mithen, *The Singing Neanderthals*. Mithen posits that "the Neanderthals used their brains for a sophisticated communication system that was Holistic, manipulative, multi-modal, musical, and mimetic in character: 'Hmmmmm.'" p. 221.

musilanguage: Steven Brown, "The 'Musilanguage' Model of Music Evolution," in *The Origins of Music*s. Brown proposes a single precursor to both language and music, a system of communication he calls *musilanguage*. He speculates that initially pitch provided a lexical reference to emotion, and this eventually gave rise to the melody of music and to the tonality of tonal languages. He surmises that the second stage involved phrase formation and expressive phrasing where language was able to provide semantic meaning, while music developed as ritualized activity that included special features such as harmony. p. 271-300.

the vaulted cave: David Elkington, *The Ancient Language of Sacred Sound*. Elkington argues for the importance of ancient sacred power places in the development of music, science, and civilizations. For example, Newgrange, a circular, monumental, multi-chambered, stone and earth burial mound in Ireland dates to about 3500 BCE and is much like an underground cathedral. Researchers from Princeton University noted that resonant frequencies were well defined and lay between 95 and 120 Hz at Newgrange and Loughcrew, also in Ireland, and at Carn Euny in Cornwall, and Wayland's Smithy in Berkshire, England. As well, rock art on the chamber walls bore some similarity to the observed resonant standing wave patterns. p. 23-26.

song of songs: *Song of Songs*, *The New Jerusalem Bible*. A transcendent account of love, nature, and song—for all lovers to read. "My love lifts up his voice, he says to me, 'Come then, my beloved, my lovely one, come. For see, winter is past, the rains are over and gone. Flowers are appearing on the earth. The season of glad songs has come.'" 1:10-12.

where music begins: Nils Wallin, Bjorn Merker, and Steven Brown, eds., *The Origins of Music*. This work presents several theories on the origins of music through an interdisciplinary lens of evolutionary biomusicology; William Thompson, *Music, Thought, and Feeling*. Thompson provides a concise review of musical origin theories based on reproductive and survival benefits, as well as a review of precursors to music. p. 19-41.

in motherese: Richard Parncutt, "Prenatal Development," *Oxford Handbook of Music Psychology*. The term refers to the playful two-way vocal and gestural interaction between infants and mothers. "Of course, men (not only fathers) and women other than mothers can and should speak motherese." p. 220. It is perhaps not music as such, but may represent music's origin, a *protomusic*.

to raise the anchor: In *Work Songs*, Ted Gioia tells of the rhythms and melodies that have accompanied tasks of all kinds down through human history. Among the many benefits, these songs rhythmically entrain workers to accomplish a physical task, provide emotional release, while helping to create community bonds.

to wind the molten string: Curt Sachs, *The History of Musical Instruments*. This classic book includes times from prehistory to the 20th century, all continents, and all stages of evolution, from primitive rattles to modern electronics—a staggering story of scientific invention coupled with artistic creativity and expression.

fingered holes in bone of bird: Philip Ball, *The Music Instinct*. "Several flutes of bone have been found from the Stone Age—that's to say, the Paleolithic period, deep into the last ice age" p. 18. One more or less complete and rather elegant flute carved from a bird, dating back to 40,000 years ago, was found in 2008 in a cave in the Swabian Jura. p. 19.

iii. the quest in question (p.8)

a story: Paul Lauzon, "Close Encounters of the Musical Kind," in *Listening, Playing, Creating: Essays on the Power of Sound*: Carolyn Kenny, ed., p. 128–36. I present this story from my clinical music therapy practice, with personal identifiers removed in respect of confidentiality.

music child: Paul Nordoff, Clive Robbins, and David Marcus, *Creative Music Therapy*. For Nordoff and Robbins the *music child* is "the individualized musicality inborn in every child: the term has reference to the universality of human musical sensitivity—the heritage of complex and subtle sensitivity to the ordering and relationship of tonal and rhythmic movement, and to the uniquely personal significance of each child's musical responsiveness." p. 3.

musicking: Christopher Small, *Musicking*. Small asserts that we can describe music not merely as a *noun/a thing*, but also as a *verb/an activity* that encompasses performing, composing, and listening—all aspects of musical engagement.

mirror ... mozaic ... mural: Each of these perspectives provides an elegant way of understanding the world: as a pure reflection of light upon ourselves; as a way of combining the many to become one; and as seeing the big picture through a lens of growth and development.

where go I on this journey of life: See Part Two of this book, *Anatomy of a Musical Being*—an extended inquiry into "why is music effective as therapy"? To get to the bottom of this question I realized I must consider music more fully by asking "what happens when music happens"? Since music and human are conjoined, I decided to link this topic of "when music happens" to three important questions for every human life: where am I going? what am I?, and what of the other? Sections iv. (I respond), v. (giving voice), and vi. (changeling) answer the question "where am I going"? (music is responsive, expressive, changing).

what am I: Sections vii. (the song of bodybrain), viii. (homage to feelings), and ix. (webs of meaning) answer the question "what am I"? (music is neuro-biological, emotive, cognitive).

what of this reaching out … to other: Sections x. (earthsong), xi. (variations on relations), and xii. (psalm for the known unknown) answer the question "what of the other"? (music is ecological, relational, transpersonal).

iv. I respond (p.11)

a hundred periodicities: György Buzsáki, *Rhythms of the Brain*. This neuroscientist addresses issues related to the genesis of brain rhythms/oscillations and their contribution to the invisible operations of the brain. See also Michael Thaut and Donald Hodges; "Rhythm, Music, and the Brain;" *The Oxford Handbook of Music and the Brain*.

infradian rhythms: Russell Foster and Leon Kreitzman; *Rhythms of Life*. "Infradian (longer than a day) rhythms time behaviours with periods of months or a year, such as migration, reproduction and hibernation." p. 2. Ernest Rossi and David Nimmons; *The 20-Minute Break*. "The best-known infradian is the rhythmic waxing and waning of the menstrual cycle in women once every twenty-eight days or so." p. 16. Another infradian cycle is seasonal affective disorder (SAD), the "winter blues" that affects one out of every ten people.

ultradian rhythms: Foster and Kreitzman; *Rhythms of Life*. Ultradian is "a biological rhythm with a period much shorter (that is, a frequency much higher) than that of a circadian rhythm; an example is the heart beat." p. 247. In *The 20-Minute Break*, Rossi and Nimmons explain that "Approximately twelve to sixteen times every day, we experience the effects of many 90 to 120 minute ultradian (more than once a day) rhythms that regulate activity and fifteen to twenty minutes of rest is considered so important that is has come to be called the *basic rest-activity cycle* (BRAC)." p. 22. These cycles are in time with many fundamental human processes "when even our muscles, glands, circulatory system, and organs resonate to it, and our very brain and psychological state keep time to it ... [and] reflect pervasive patterns of communication between our mind and body." p. 24.

circadian rhythms: Foster and Kreitzman; *Rhythms of Life*. Circadian is "a biological rhythm that persists under constant conditions with a period length of around a day." p. 245. "Daily circadian rhythms (*circa*, about; *diem*, a day) are orchestrated by a central clock to keep our bodily systems working in harmony." p. 2. Examples include: kidney function, body temperature, heart rate, blood pressure, cognitive abilities, pain sensitivity, hormone production, and many more. p. 11.

beta to alpha frequencies: The EEG (electroencephalograph) measures brainwaves of different frequencies within the brain: Gamma greater than 30(Hz), Beta (13-30Hz), Alpha (8-12 Hz), Theta (4-8 Hz), and Delta (less than 4 Hz). Binaural music is used to help individuals lower brain frequency from beta (alert conscious mind) to the more meditative alpha frequencies. When listening to two tones, each at a different frequency and each in a different ear, your brain creates an additional tone you can hear. This third tone is a binaural beat. In *The Rhythmic Language of Health and Disease*, Mark Rider points to the harmonic organization of the central nervous system; "In our own lab, we have observed that in cycles per second (Hz), alpha is twice theta, and beta is twice alpha. If, for example, theta is 5 Hz, then alpha is 10 Hz and beta is 20 Hz. Delta may very well represent the first peak, or fundamental frequency." p. 35.

bardic voices as they pitch: Paul Lauzon; "Folk song as a therapeutic resource." "In his meta-analysis of folk song, ethno-musicologist Alan Lomax suggested that there are ten or more musical style families in the world—American Indian, Pygmoid, African,

Australian, Melanesian, Polynesian, Malayan, Eurasian, Old European, and Modern European (including the Americas). R. Cohen ed., *Alan Lomax: Selected Writings*. "It seems clear that these ten styles have spread over large areas during extremely long periods of time, possibly with the diffusion of the modern races of mankind. They appear to change more slowly than any other human art." p. 167. "Between the extremes of the solo unaccompanied and the contrapuntal styles, Lomax outlined what he called the bardic style, found primarily in Eurasia." (Lauzon) "The Oriental bard is a highly idiosyncratic solo singer, a master of subtly designed verse and of complex, shifting, and sometimes meterless rhythm." (Lomax, p. 265). "These singers are accompanied by various instruments. One of Lomax's primary conclusions was that interpersonal relationships and role-taking tend to mirror a society's singing style." (Lauzon)

the storm of epic song: Albert Bates Lord; *The Singer of Tales* (2nd edition, 2000). Lord explains the processes of composition of oral narrative poetry, particularly the Iliad and Odyssey of Homer, and the performance art of the epic singers of Yugoslavia, circa 1920-40's. He describes the special techniques and formulas of composition which make *rapid composing in performance* possible. "We believe that the epic singers from the dawn of human consciousness have been a deeply significant group and have contributed abundantly to the spiritual and intellectual growth of man." Foreword, p. xxxv. In *The Hidden Ireland*, Daniel Corkery explains that in the Celtic bardic schools, students were given a subject suitable to their capacities. "The said Subject having been given over Night, they worked it apart each by himself upon his own Bed, the whole next day in the Dark, till at a certain Hour in the Night, lights being brought in, they committed it to writing ... and come together into a large Room, where the Masters waited, each Scholar gave in his Performance," p. 74. The bardic training was years long and arduous, each bard highly trained in his poetic craft and able to discharge "his knowledge of the history and tradition of his country and his clan." p. 77. These schools survived from the 5th to the 18th century in Ireland.

v. giving voice (p.15)

I hear the voice of others: Don Ihde; *Listening and Voice.* This book presents a detailed phenomenology of many aspects of sound by a philosopher who is well-grounded in the science and experience of the auditory, vocal, and listening dimensions. "Yet all sounds are in a broad sense 'voices,' the voices of things, of others, of the gods, and of myself... the voices of language." p. 147.

I am born into a language: Joseph Flanagan; *Quest for Self-Knowledge.* "Our present cultural identity as knowers, choosers, and lovers depends on the historical situation in which we were born and the linguistic community in which and through which our experiences have been, and are being lived and mediated. Any linguistic community will have a history of past knowing, choosing, and loving which has advanced and/or obscured and blocked the transcending identity of past cultural communities." p. 15.

in this language a music: Aniruddh Patel; *Music, Language, and the Brain.* "These explorations indicate that music and language should be seen as complex constellations of sub-processes, some of which are shared, and others not... As cognitive and neural systems, music and language are closely related. Comparing music and language provides a powerful way to study the mechanisms that the mind uses to make sense out of sound." p. 417.

a witness, a presence: George Steiner; *Real Presences.* "Both intuitively and theoretically, Western speculation on the psychology of aesthetic reception, from Plato to Freud and Jung, has been drawn towards intimations of *re*-cognition, of *déja-vu* and *déja-entendu*. We have met before." p. 180.

as you reach from inner to outer speech: Don Ihde; *Listening and Voice.* Ihde provides an elegant description and explanation of the polyphony of inner and outer voice and of the importance of voice in how we perceive the world. "Voice is, for us humans, a very central phenomenon. It bears our language without which we would perceive differently. Yet outward from this center, voice may also be a perspective, a metaphor, by which we understand part of the world itself. For metaphor is to language what perspective is to perception, and both are integral to the way in which we experience things." p. 189.

vi. changeling (p.17)

to the beating of her heart: Richard Parncutt; "Prenatal Development," *Oxford Handbook of Music Psychology.* "The human fetus has access to three behavioural sources of information about maternal state: sound patterns, linear and rotational acceleration of the fetal body, and relative movement of the fetal limbs. These are perceived by the fetal auditory, vestibular, and proprioceptive systems respectively." p. 224. "Hearing may be regarded as the dominant sensory modality in the prenatal phase ... The cochlea begins to process sounds at about around 20 weeks gestation; the cochlea reaches adult size at 25 weeks, but continues to develop until birth." p. 220.

a lullaby of freedom: Sandra Trehub; *Music Lessons from Infants.* "Although music for adults often differs substantially from one culture to another, music for infants has many cross-cultural similarities. For example, lullabies from foreign musical cultures are readily recognizable as such, perhaps by virtue of common features such as simplicity, repetitiveness, and falling pitch contours." p. 229.

as swing the limbs of change: John Russon; *Bearing Witness to Epiphany.* "The child grows. What the child grows into is a *world* ... The experience of growth is characterized by the experience of the growing sense of "I" (among other things), and the sense of "I" is fundamentally a sense of "I can" ... The growing significance of the "I can" that derives from the child's "own body" is matched by a growing richness to things — the common fabric they weave grows more complex and systematic, and the individual things themselves develop greater consistency—and a growing integration with other people, who themselves take on more clearly defined personalities. Reality simultaneously becomes more deeply differentiated and more tightly interwoven, denser and more articulate, rhythmically and harmonically more rich and melodically more intricate." p. 50.

spells like scars remain: Paul Watzlawick, John H. Weakland, and Richard Fisch; *Change: Principles of Problem Formation and Problem Resolution.* These authors "have studied the ways in which problems are created and maintained by wrong attempts at solving a difficulty … the target of change is the attempted solution; and the tactic chosen has to be translated into the person's own 'language;' that is, it must be presented to him in a form which utilizes his own way of conceptualizing 'reality.'" p. 109–112. Wise words.

assert the one you keep becoming: Bernard Lonergan; *The Subject.* "For we are subjects, as it were, by degrees … unconscious in dreamless sleep … helpless subjects of our dreams … experiential subjects when we awake … intelligent subjects when we inquire about our experience, investigate, grow in understanding … rational subjects when we question our own understanding, judge this to be so and that not to be so … self-conscious subjects when we deliberate, evaluate, decide, act. Then there emerges human consciousness at its fullest. Then the existential subject exists and his character, his personal essence, is at stake." p. 69.

and I a changing self am music changing: Paul Lauzon, "Anatomy of a Musical Being." "Some music states are correlated to personal growth." section 1.3.3.

vii. the song of bodybrain (p.21)

as signals at speed of light: Thenille Janzen and Michael Thaut; *Cerebral Organization of Music Processing.* Neuroimaging research has identified several regions of the brain involved in music processing. "Interactions between auditory and frontal cortical areas are crucial for ... tonal context, for the integration of sound events over time in working memory ... in autobiographical memories, attention, and musical imagery;"..."coordination between auditory and motor-related areas ... are involved in sensorimotor coordination and temporal processing;"..."Auditory and limbic interactions ... in relation to affective sound processing and music-evoked emotions"; "[research] literature suggests that music processing requires timely coordination of large-scale cognitive, motor, and limbic brain networks." p. 89.

reptilian brain: Patrick Steffen, Dawson Hedges and Rebekka Matheson; *The Brain is Adaptive not Triune*. These authors build on Paul MacLean's original Triune Brain theory. They acknowledge that the human brain has evolved over time (reptilian/brain stem, pre-mammalian/limbic, and mammalian/cortex), but suggest that these areas are interdependent and adaptive. "A primary function of the brain is to make adaptive models of the external and internal environments. Current findings indicate that brain function is based on interdependent networks ... In particular, the brain appears to work by integrating interoceptive and exteroceptive information to make predictions about future metabolic, energy, and other needs while it adapts to continually changing external and internal conditions to maintain homeostasis and to initiate allostasis as needed." p. 9.

your left brain chants her mastery of sequence: Although the two hemispheres of the brain function differently, they work together and complement each other, whatever function you perform, you receive input from both sides. Generally speaking, the left hemisphere handles sequential/serial information very well. The right brain handles synchronous/harmonious information very well. See Iain McGilchrist; *The Master and His Emissary*, for a modern classic that explains "It is not *what* each hemisphere does, but *how* it does it that matters. Each hemisphere is involved in everything, true enough; just in a quite different way." p. x

you shift both night and day: Mark Rider; *The Rhythmic Language.* In counterpoint to the theory of metabolic balance called *homeostasis*, Rider points to the importance of what he calls a theory of *homeodynamism.* "... no physical changes occur without these mental/electrical shifts occurring. Furthermore, health is associated with a particular rhythm of shifting which is related to normal human and cosmic rhythms. Disease states follow conditions in which this healthy rhythm has been altered or eliminated altogether ... [and] that mind and body are organized in the same way, permitting total bodymind communication." p. 3.

hope to find the slippery mind: Ian Ravenscroft; *Philosophy of Mind.* "It's one thing to give neurological explanations of the various relationships between our [music] experiences; it's quite another to explain the [music] experiences *themselves.*" p. 185. There remains the *explanatory gap* between brain states and phenomenal experiences, between the objective and the subjective. In understanding the human mind/consciousness, one must go beyond brain research as interpreted in a strict reductionist manner to include a more inclusive philosophical perspective.

viii. homage to feelings (p.24)

and quietly the cat: Marc Bekoff; "Animal Emotions: Exploring Passionate Natures." This article asserts that interdisciplinary research provides compelling evidence that many animals experience such emotions as joy, fear, love, despair, and grief.

drives of thirst and loneliness: Agnes Heller, *A Theory of Feelings.* "I feel — I am involved in something. This 'something' can be anything: another human being, a concept, myself, a process, a problem, a situation, another feeling, another involvement." p. 11. From this beginning, Heller develops a phenomenology of feeling that includes the nature of feeling itself in distinct categories of drives, affects, emotions, emotional dispositions, moods, orientive feelings, and passions.

in my sanguine tempers: Even though modern medical science has rejected the ancient theory of the *four temperaments* (that there are four fundamental personality types: sanguine, choleric, melancholic, and phlegmatic), they persist as useful metaphors when discussing types in certain psychological contexts and have been adapted by thinkers such as Immanuel Kant, Alfred Adler, and Erich Fromm.

of music and tears you ask: Patrik Juslin and John Sloboda; *Music and Emotion.* This text provides a multidisciplinary review of theory and research of a topic that has intrigued thinkers throughout human history.

your sad and lonely song of love: It seems a simple thing, but what really happens when you are listening to a sad song? Stephen Davies, in *Philosophical Perspectives*, points out that "our experiences of artworks educate us about the emotions in a setting that insulates us from the practical demands and dangers of the real world ... its negative aspects are transformed to positive ones through the delight taken in the narrative's construction, the natural attractiveness of representation, and so on ... It simply is not true that people always duck the avoidable negative aspects of life. These are recognized as essential components of many things we like and value ... people willingly engage with something so rewarding as music, though they know that doing so will expose them to expressions of negative emotions, which are liable to cause feelings that are unpleasant to experience." p. 40-42.

a thought performed in pleasure or in pain: Malcolm Budd; *Music and the Emotions.* Budd provides a model of "emotion as a thought experienced with pleasure or pain" and points out that emotions can have opposites, they can be mixed, are not necessarily revealed in a person's outward appearance. There are many ways an emotion can be manifested in one's behaviour, and generally "a person's happiness is a function of the kinds of emotion that fill his life." p. 14-15.

catharsis: A sense of cleansing, of purging emotions, particularly through drama or music.

ix. webs of meaning (p.28)

hear a music in the words: Poets study *prosody*, the musical sounds of words — accents, meters, patterns of verse and such. Musical philosophers ask how we can use words to explain the *meaning of the music itself*, without the help of lyrics. Donald Hodges in *A Concise Survey of Music Philosophy* outlines the three primary theories on how music has meaning: "The first dichotomy involves a question of whether the meaning and value of music is found in the music itself [*Absolutists*] or in what music points to outside itself [*Referentialists*]." P. 81. "... *expressionists* find meaning and value in the musical expression of feelings and emotions." p. 84.

bring family 'round communal fire: Ian Cross; "Music in recent evolutionary thought." Cross explains that there are three identifiable areas in which music has proved to be of essential importance in the evolution of humankind. 1) The "coordinating/ interactive" function of music "involves overt action and active group engagement, and is employed not only in caregiver-infant interaction, entertainment and courtship but also in ritual, particularly at times of significant life transitions (such as the passage from adolescence to adulthood, from season to season, of from life to death). More often than not, music is an integral part of a wider range of everyday activities." p. 6. 2) The function of "rhythmic entrainment refers to the coordination in time of one participant's behaviours with those of another and involves the organization of perception and behaviour around temporal regularities that are inferred (generally not consciously) from musical sounds and actions in the form of a periodic pulse or beat that is sensed by all participants." p. 6. 3) The function of "floating intentionality." "Meaning in music appears to be less susceptible to consensual determination than is meaning in language; music certainly bears meaning, but the meanings that it can bear are more impenetrable and susceptible to change according to the contexts in which they are experienced than are those of language." p. 7.

raven's song of creation: In *The Red Swan*, John Bierhorst explains that the primary purpose for a mythical creation story is for "setting the world in order." p. 4. In *The Indians' Book*, pioneering ethnomusicologist, Natalie Curtis has compiled a book where "The songs and stories are theirs; the drawings and titlepages were made by them. The work of the recorder has been but the collecting, editing, and arranging of contributions." p. x. She presents a working model for honouring and helping to preserve another culture's songs and stories beyond "cultural appropriation."

music sounds as feelings feel: Suzanne Langer; *Philosophy in a New Key*. For Langer, music is a tonal analogue, a kind of symbolic presentation of how we experience feelings, as in the tension/release of musical movement. "Not communication but insight is the gift of music; in a very naive phrase, a knowledge of 'how feelings go.'" p. 244.

way out beyond the five: Why does music work this way? Is it an analogue for life? We start at the *one* (C) and journey out as far as we can go to the *five* (G), until eventually through permutations and modulations we wind back to home base, to the *one*. Is the *five* our Jungian "shadow self"? Shall we consider the *twelve* a turnaround in 12 bar blues — or perhaps a complete 12 tone chromatic scale?

time is the now of being changing: Bernard Lonergan; *Topics in Education*. "Fundamental thought about time in St. Thomas [Aquinas] is in terms of the *nunc*. Eternity is the 'now' that has no change, the 'now' of a being that does not change; and time is the 'now' of a being that does change." p. 227.

rounded tone to interval: One way of considering music as a "language" is to compare music with verbal language through the discipline of linguistics: basic sounds can be seen as tones or phonemes; grammar understood as generative musical structure compared to verbal syntax; semantics as music or words having meaning. Similarities can be found. Major differences include the fact that words have *specific semantic meaning* and can be translated, whereas music cannot. Music has *tonal harmony* as syntactical structure, whereas words are ordinarily meant to be sounded one at a time.

blending into fugue: Robert K. Barnhart; *Chambers Dictionary of Etymology.* "fugue n. a musical composition based on short themes that are interwoven; borrowed from Italian *fuga*, literally, flight." p. 413.

x. earthsong (p.32)

Gaia opens her soul: In Greek mythology Gaia was Earth personified as a goddess, daughter of Chaos, mother and wife of Uranus (Heaven). In 1969, *Gaia: A New Look at Life on Earth* by British scientist, James Lovelock, put forward the hypothesis that the Earth functions as a vast self-regulating entity, such that the entire range of living matter on the earth collectively defines and regulates the material conditions necessary for the continuance of life.

the orchestra is tuning: Bernie Krause; *The Great Animal Orchestra.* "Bioacoustics" is a cross-disciplinary science investigating the production, dispersion, and reception of sound in all living creatures, in air, on land, in sea. The findings provide clues about the evolution of acoustic mechanisms and, from that, the evolution of animals that employ them. Krause offers the idea that music originated in the sound-communication systems of wild animals.

to breech above the ocean laughing: Roger Payne; *Among Whales.* "These [humpback whale] songs ... can last up to thirty minutes, though fifteen is nearer the norm. They are divided into repeating phrases called themes. When the phrase is heard to change (usually after a few minutes), it heralds the start of a new theme. Songs contain from two to nine themes and are strung together without pauses so that a long singing session is an exuberant, uninterrupted river of sound that can flow on for twenty-four hours or longer. The pace of the song is very grand and extended and appears to me to be set by the slow rhythm of ocean swells—the rhythm of the sea." p. 144. "Humpback whales [53 million years] and humans have been on separate but parallel paths of evolution since long before the appearance of our earliest hominid ancestors [100,000 years] ... yet whales use many of the same laws of composition in their songs that we use in ours ... similar rhythms ... phrases of a similar length ... even though they are capable of singing over a range of at least seven octaves, humpback whales use intervals between their notes similar to the intervals that we employ in our scales ... mix percussive or noisy elements in their songs with relatively pure tones, and mix them in ratios similar to the ratios humans use in symphonic music ... overall song structure is similar to human compositions—a statement of them, a section in which it is elaborated (the development section), and then a return to a slightly modified version of the original theme ... the quality of many whale notes is the same as the quality of human notes ... humpbacks employ rhyme in their songs." p. 146-147. "This commonality of aesthetic suggests to me that the traditions of singing may date back so far they were already present in some ancestor common to whales and us." p.166.

xi. variations on my relations (p.35)

variations: Alan Belkin; *Musical Composition.* "Variation form is by nature a challenge to the imagination ... the composer has to find ways to create contrasting, novel surfaces that renew interest, even as the underlying skeleton is repeated multiple times." p. 91.

"Within each variation the character normally remains fairly stable. Each variation is a distinct piece, with its own character, and there is usually a high degree of motivic homogeneity. Significant changes normally occur only between variations." p. 91-92.

on my relations: J. Krishnamurti; *On Relationship.* "To understand the complexity of relationship there must be thoughtful patience and earnestness. Relationship is a process of self-revelation in which one discovers the hidden causes of sorrow. This self-revelation is only possible in relationship." p. 3. "The understanding of the world begins with the understanding of ourselves. The problem is not the world, but you in relationship with another, which creates a problem; and that problem extended becomes the world problem." p. 26.

mother, if I do not cry: Words can echo feelings — in this case mourning — as something buried in the music of the sounds themselves.

ignite aeolian strings: *Aeolus* was Latin god of the winds. An Aeolian harp is placed outdoors where the wind can easily blow through and vibrate the strings, creating an improvised (improvisus: unforeseen) music that is carried by the wind. The Aeolian mode is our natural minor 7-step scale of tone, semitone, tone, tone, semitone, tone, tone.

Celtic knots on head of drum: *Cymatics,* as developed by Hans Jenny, is the study of how sound is made visible as wave patterns in sand when a plate, diaphragm, or membrane is vibrated. Different patterns emerge, reminiscent of the mandala and other forms recurring in nature. The frequency spectrum of the signal that excites the vibration determines which patterns are nodally displayed.

akashic songbook: Ervin Laszlo; *Science and the Akashic Field.* Ervin Laszlo names the *in-formation field of nature* the *Akashic* *field*. "In the Sanskrit and Indian cultures, Akasha is an all-encompassing medium that underlies all things and becomes all things." p 76. "The Akashic vision of a cyclic universe — of a Metaverse that creates universe after universe — is essentially the vision we now get from cosmology … It is the original field out of which emerged particles and atoms, stars and planets, human and animal bodies, and all the things that can be seen and touched. It is a dynamic, energy-filled medium in ceaseless fluctuation." p. 77.

songs of paddling: There are many wonderful canoeing songs found in French Canada (my heritage). Edith Fowke in *Chansons de Québec* comments that one paddling song "was probably composed by a shanty-boy rejoicing in the prospect of joining his family and friends after spending a winter in the woods." p. 11. Fowke, in *Canadian Folk Songs*, explains that the two largest groups of Canadian songs are "those composed by men who worked on the sea or in the woods." p. 12. Rivers were the highways and byways into Canada and the canoe was the chosen vehicle.

xii. psalm to the known unknown (p.39)

an altered state of mind: Ronald Havens; *The Wisdom of Milton H. Erickson*. Havens summarizes Erickson's observations on the unconscious mind [what he sometimes referred to as *useful unrealized self-knowledge*]. "It sees things the conscious mind ignores, it knows things the conscious mind overlooks, and it remembers things the conscious mind has forgotten." p. 64. "It contains a vast range of unrecognized capabilities and potentials … Diverse cultural backgrounds do not seem to prevent clear communication and understanding at the unconscious level of awareness." p. 65.

communitas: Edith Turner; *Communitas*. "Communitas often appears unexpectedly. It has to do with the sense felt by a group of people when their life together takes on full meaning … occurs through the readiness of the people — perhaps from necessity — to rid themselves of their concern for status and dependence on structures, and see their fellows as they are." p. 1. "It often comes in the direst moments of the life of a person or society... Communitas dwells with the powers of the weak... Communitas is a group's pleasure in sharing common experiences with one's fellows." p. 2.

organ pipe to shake the nave: Another of Johann Sebastian Bach's many accomplishments was the design, re-building, and maintenance of large pipe organs. See Christoph Wolff, *Johann Sebastian Bach. p.* 142-145.

by Manifestation: John Hatcher; *The Face of God Among Us.* The Bahá'í Faith presents an argument for progressive revelation. "... these specialized Emissaries [Buddha, Krishna, Zoroaster, Moses, Jesus Christ, Muhammad, Bahá'u'lláh] are not ordinary human beings, but an order of representatives from the divine realm Who perfectly incarnate or *manifest* all the attributes of God but are not of the same *essence* as God — that is, They are not incarnations of God Himself, but of His qualities ... each successive Manifestation *seals up* or is the *end* or culmination of all that has gone before, and yet is the *beginning* of a new revelation, another stage in human development." p. 76-77.

circling round the Lote tree: Also known as *Sidr tree, Christ's Thorn, Jujube or Nabk tree.* The botanical name is *Ziziphus spina-christi.* It is an ancient tree with many nourishing and healing properties.

a God who dances: Ananda Coomaraswamy; *The Dance of Shiva.* "Whatever the origins of Shiva's dance, it became in time the clearest image of the *activity* of God which any art or religion can boast of." p. 52. "In the night of Brahma, Nature is inert, and cannot dance till Shiva wills it: He rises from His rapture, and dancing sends through inert matter pulsing waves of awakening sound, and lo! matter also dances appearing as a glory round about Him. Dancing, He sustains its manifold phenomena. In the fullness of time, still dancing, He destroys all forms and names by fire and gives new rest. This is poetry; but none the less, science." p. 62.

music calls me to vocation: Literally from the Latin *vocare* to call. Interesting how one's path in life, one's occupation or profession, is connected to the voice, to this sense of being called to one's true calling.

modulation: W. A. Mathieu; *Harmonic Experience.* "Modulation is a shift from one tonal center to another, a 'change of key.' p. 253. "But the ancient modal modulations and the complex modulations of modern tonal harmony are based on the same principle: Harmonic continuity allows modulation to be sensible—just as any two tones ... any two triads ... so will any two keys be heard as closely related if the tonics are distant by a fifth." p. 255.

of our deepest yearnings: 1 Samuel 16:23; "And whenever the spirit from God came over Saul, David would take a harp and play; Saul would then be soothed; it would do him good, and the evil spirit would leave him."

Shaker and Sufi in their turnings: The Shakers are members of an American Christian sect named for the ecstatic whirling and shaking engaged in by its members. Sufism is the inner spiritual path of the Islamic faith. One Sufi sect is the *whirling dervish* order, famous for their circling dances as a way to mystical union with God.

Cistercian monk: The Cistercian order was founded in 1098 at Citeaux near Dijon in France with a mission to follow the strict contemplative monastic rule of St. Benedict. The monks live in vocal silence, but for the singing of daily and seasonal prayers and hymns seven times each day. The *Kyrie* is a short repeated invocation, part of the Roman Catholic Mass. *Kyrie eleison* is Greek for *Lord, have mercy.*

the war torn in their cellar: Karl Rahner; *The Need and the Blessing of Prayer.* In a sermon given in the bombed-out ruins of St. Michael's Church in Munich in the winter of 1946, Karl Rahner reminds his congregation,; "Do you remember the nights in the cellar, the nights of deadly loneliness amidst the harrowing crush of people? The nights when the lights went out, when horror and impotence gripped one's heart, when one mimed being courageous and unaffected? When one's innocently bold and brave words sounded so strangely wooden and empty, as if they were already dead before they even reached the other person? When one finally gave up, when one became silent, when one only waited hopelessly for the end, death? Alone, powerless, empty." p. 3. For the people, war in reality is not the war of glory—when even the bravest words are empty of effect.

xiii. this particular I (p.42)

natural system first: For Ludwig von Bertalanffy in *General System Theory* (GST), a system is either isolated from its environment (*closed system*), or continuously exchanging matter/energy with its environment (*open system*). As an open system, a *natural system* is one that does not owe its existence to conscious human planning and execution. GST has identified these four organizational features common to natural systems: 1) ordered wholeness, 2) maintenance of steady-state, 3) self-reorganization in the face of challenge, and 4) hierarchical fit in a multi-holon reality.

an irreducible ordered whole: 1) *Natural systems are wholes with irreducible properties.* The four features of natural systems as presented in the poem are more fully explained in the accompanying essay *Anatomy of a Musical Being*, section 2.3 *Natural Systems.*

self-monitoring and repairing: 2) *Natural Systems maintain themselves in a changing environment.*

when challenged by loss: 3) *Natural Systems create themselves in response to the challenge of the environment.*

part of larger wholes: 4) *Natural Systems are coordinating interfaces in nature's hierarchy.*

natural musical systems: Joseph Flanagan; *Quest for Self-Knowledge.* "A chief characteristic of a system is the range of questions that it is able to incorporate and bring under control. But as the system develops, it tends to become more specialized, clarifying its own boundaries, thereby setting the conditions for new transcending questions which will eventually incorporate and comprehend more extensively transcending operations and fields of interest." p. 14.

rhythmos tonos harmonia: Paul Lauzon; *Materia Musica or a Philosophy of Music as Therapy.* Since 1992, I have been working with the idea that we are wired for sound, that we have musical systems. "It will be argued that, as a structural system, music is a unique formal force able to invigorate and to potentialize the wholeness of a person, and hence, of mankind. In order to speak of rhythm, tone, and harmony in a more humanly activated manner, I have chosen to use the words "rhythmos, "tonos" and "harmonia." These terms refer to musical events, qualities, and capacities within the human being. The *rhythmos* is that which makes the individual a rhythmic being. The *tonos* is that which makes the person a tonal being. The *harmonia* is that which makes the individual a harmonious being." p. 67.

xiv. rhythmos (p.45)

rhythmos: The natural musical system that makes the individual a rhythmic being, manifest in the basic periodicities and cycles of a human life.

121

pineal gland of sparrow: Foster and Kreitzman; *Rhythms of Life.*
"The pineal had to contain a clock because the transplanted pineal
[of sparrow] carried with it a critical component of any clock, its
phase. This was the first time [1979] that a circadian clock had been
clearly localised to a part of the brain in any vertebrate." p. 125.

time their floral rendezvous: Foster and Keitzman; *Rhythms of
Life.* "Despite this mechanistic simplicity, these humble little bees
have an innate ability to work out the location of a food source
from its position in relation to the sun; they do this even on cloudy
days by reading the pattern of the polarisation of the light, and
pass this information to other bees. The bees can communicate
how far away the food is up to a distance of about 15 kilometres."
p. 27; "[the bee] has a circadian clock that is reset daily to run
with the solar cycle. The bee can consult this clock and 'check'
off the given time and associate this with a particular event, such
as orange blossom at 10.00, lavender at 12.00. It seems that bees
know how to tell the time." p. 28.

suprachiasmatic nuclei: Known as the SCN, this small, paired
cluster of 20,000 cells in the anterior hypothalamus has been
identified as the mammalian master pacemaker, the localised
source of most circadian timings. Locating this anatomical
substrate of specific rhythmic behavioural control systems is a
remarkable achievement of neuroscientific research.

of great complexity and reach: 1) *Ordered wholeness is essential to
rhythmos.* The four natural system aspects of *rhythmos* as presented
in the poem are more fully explained in the accompanying essay
Anatomy of a Musical Being, section 2.4.1 *Rhythmos.*

in balance of endeavour: 2) *Rhythmos is an open system in steady
state.*

rhythmos a force for change: 3) *Rhythmos has the capacity for
creative self-reorganization in the face of challenge.*

on to pulse and gathering cycles: 4) *Rhythmos is a coordinating interface in a hierarchical structure.*

slowly running waves of structure: Process in human musical *rhythmos* is similar to process in our physiological systems; both are sustained by an underlying hierarchy of forms, often working together; for example, when the pre-formed ventricle structure of the heart supports its function of rhythmic contraction.

xv. tonos (p.48)

tonos: *Tonos* is that music system which organizes humans as sound generating beings, particularly through the voice. We know the voice is deeply connected to feelings, and that vocal sounds express the wide range of emotion. The four natural system aspects of *tonos* as presented in the poem are more fully explained in the accompanying essay *Anatomy of a Musical Being*, section 2.4.2 *Tonos*.

in voice and ear to auditory cortex: 1) *Tonos is a system with ordered wholeness.*

breath supports this voice: 2) *Tonos maintains itself in a changing environment.*

resets the drone of natural pitch: 3) *Tonos creates itself in a changing environment.*

invariant law of nature: 4) *Tonos is a coordinating interface in a hierarchical reality.*

our own instrument: From the first cry of birth, each one of us is gifted with a musical instrument, the one to which all other instruments refer—the voice.

xvi. harmonia (p.51)

harmonia: W. K. C. Guthrie; *Presocratics and the Pythagoreans.* For the ancient Greeks, the word *harmonia* meant "the joining or fitting of things together, even the material peg with which they were joined, then especially the stringing of an instrument with strings of different tautness, and so a musical scale." p. 220. Harmony brings together all other aspects of music, particularly rhythm and melody. The music system called *harmonia* easily takes on the four attributes common to all natural systems.

the monochord of Aristides: David Creese; *The Monochord.* The early Greeks were keen to study the many connections of music and geometry/mathematics, particularly *mathematical harmonics.* Concerning the monochord, Creese explores these pertinent questions; "What, if anything, is unique about the way it mediates between the sensory and intelligible realms … what effect does this have on the way it was used by Greek harmonicists, and on the development of their scientific methods"? p. 10.

doh sol a perfect fifth: W. A. Mathieu; *Harmonic Experience.* "It is not enough to listen passively to pure harmonies, or learn to recognize them, or to combine them on an instrument. One has to connect them with one's feelings by placing them in the body. Sung harmony is embodied intelligence." p. 4. Concerning the study of music theory, he says; "What if your heart is singing fortissimo and your mind is bored to tears? Then you realize that your mind needs to sing too. I think you find the balance between heart and mind by asking your heart what it really needs to become musically complete." p. 6.

a vertical stacking of tones: 1) *Harmonia is a whole with irreducible properties.* The four natural system aspects of *harmonia* as presented in the poem are more fully explained in the accompanying essay *Anatomy of a Musical Being*, section 2.4.3 *Harmonia.*

expanding our sense of consonance: 2) *Harmonia maintains in a changing environment.*

find new tolerances of dissonance: Interestingly, the development of tonal harmony in Western music coincides with the developmental structure of the harmonic series (fundamental and rising overtones). Intervals that once were rejected became able to be heard and accepted: 1) in Greek music and early Gregorian chant we hear unison singing in octaves (C C'); 2) from CE. 850, singing of *organum* in parallel 4ths and 5ths (C F and C G); 3) from CE. 1400, using major and minor *triads* (C E G and C Eb G); 4) from CE. 1600, addition of the chordal 7th(C E G Bb); 5) from CE. 1750, addition of the chordal 9th(C E G Bb D); 6) from CE. 1880, use of the whole tone scale (Bb C D E F#); and 7) early 1900s CE. total chromaticism and 12-tone technique, as well as experimentation with microtones.

the pulling apart and scrambling on to unity: 3) *Harmonia creates in response to the challenge of the environment.*

we seek and find harmonia: 4) *Harmonia is a coordinating interface in nature's hierarchy.*

smiling in her many faces: The unfolding of the following examples of harmony were inspired by Paul Kuntz's interpretation in *Whitehead's Category of Harmony.* "Harmony is a metaphorical term, the meaning must change from one level to another. Things of different sorts are related by different principles ... I propose that we consider the kinds of harmony we commonly speak of under nine heads. I arrived at these nine empirically by thinking of the kinds represented in the English language. It may be more than a coincidence that John Milton celebrated a ninefold harmony." p. 2-3. In *Adventures of Ideas*, Alfred North Whitehead presents many generative ideas concerning harmony. "Thus, in its broadest sense, art is civilization. For civilization is nothing other than the unremitting aim at the major perfections of harmony." p. 271.

negotiating in rituals of living: As Joseph Flanagan points out in *Quest for Self-knowledge,* "Our cultural habits are not primarily habits of the mind, but habits of the heart; they express the attitudes and motivating meanings of our behaviour. Thus, to appropriate our cultural identity, we need to critically interpret and evaluate the cultural meanings and values we have inherited." p. 10.

in harmonia of self-identity: For John Russon, in *Bearing Witness to Epiphany,* "Like melodies, harmonies have a kind of narrative, a kind of sequentiality, but these harmonies are the structuring narratives that I have settled into, the grounding interpretations of my life to which I am habituated, rather than matters that are of explicit attention and choice in my daily affairs." p. 21-22.

one voice singing a full chord: As practiced by Tibetan Buddhist monks, the human voice is capable of "overtone singing" whereby one voice generates a lower fundamental frequency as well as moveable overtones, and these simultaneously adding psychoacoustical combination tones to form a triadic chord.

in harmonia I include: The reader may wish to consider these pertinent questions in developing their own understanding of *harmonia*: Does your consideration of *harmony* take the correlative *disharmony* into account? Does your view assume one and only one meaning? Does your thinking assume one and only one principle of harmony applying to all actual occasions? Do you assume final perfect satisfaction of one ideal?

xvii. therapeía (p.55)

therapeía: From the Greek, this term carries the double meaning of curing and healing. Curing (Latin cūra) refers to the actual medical care or treatment arising from concern. Healing (Old English hælan) is a process of making *whole* or *sound*, and arises from within the person. As Peregrine Horden asserts in

Music as Medicine: The History of Music Therapy since Antiquity, "At various times and in various cultures over the past two and a half millennia—probably still further back in time—music has been medicine." p. 1. For a collaborative account by a group of scholars whose goal is to promote interdisciplinary and cross-cultural discussion of the healing powers of music, refer to *Musical Healing in Cultural Contexts*, edited by Penelope Gouk. The burgeoning area of *medical ethnomusicology* is "a new field of integrative research and applied practice that explores holistically the roles of music and sound phenomena and related praxes in any cultural and clinical context of health and healing." *The Oxford Handbook of Medical Ethnomusicology*, edited by Benjamin Koen, is a confluence of medicine, ethnology, and music.

ancient tempered imitation: Aristotle, in *Politics*, asserts that music imitates emotion and can therefore bring about a *catharsis*—a purgation of the emotions, particularly destructive ones: "But rhythms and melodies contain representations of anger and mildness, and also of courage and temperance and all their opposites and the other moral qualities, that most closely correspond to the true natures of these qualities (and this is clear from the facts of what occurs—when we listen to such representations we change in our soul)." Music therapists speak of the "Iso Principle," as in *using music to match the person's mood*. A utilization of what the individual brings to the session is an effective clinical approach. However, the way music actually expresses emotion can vary significantly from culture to culture, so that theories based on *imitation/catharsis* are limited in their capacity for explaining *why music is effective as therapy*.

or is music a bridge: In the history of modern music therapy, it was natural that the effectiveness of music as therapy was initially explained through the heuristic of the major psychological theories of the day—psychoanalytic, behavioural, humanistic, cognitive, neurological, and their many off-shoots. In these *interpersonal theories*, music is seen as providing a bridge—an experience — wherein a therapist can establish a relationship with a client as determined by each psychological theory, and that's *why music is effective as therapy*. In *Defining Music Therapy*, Kenneth Bruscia states: "Music therapy is a systematic process of intervention wherein the therapist helps the client to promote health, using music experiences and the relationships that develop though them as dynamic forces of change." p.20.

made as music is made: As I argue in Part Two of this book, "Anatomy of a Musical Being," humans are musical beings, made as music is made, wired for sound. In the same way, we have basic bodily systems such as the circulatory or the respiratory system, we can speak analogically and anatomically as having musical systems — for example, when we speak of our rhythmic system, *rhythmos*. For Paul Nordoff and Clive Robbins, in *Creative Music Therapy*, "The Music Child is that entity in every child which responds to musical experience, finds it meaningful and engaging, remembers music, and enjoys some form of musical expression. The Music Child is therefore the individualized musicality inborn in each child." p 1. (The *Musical Being* is the *Music Child* become an adult.) Kenneth Aigen, in *Music-Centered Music Therapy*, argues "for the inherent clinical value of musical experience." p. 165. He asserts "it is the nature of how music is experienced and conceptualized that is the element most common to all types of music therapy, rather than the specifics of behavioural theory or neurological processes. And this in turn makes a strong case for the viability of music-centered concepts as a source for general theory in music therapy." p. 164. In *Frames of Mind*, Howard Gardner argues for the reality of *musical intelligence*: "The core operations of music do not bear intimate connections to the core operations in other areas; and therefore, music deserves to be considered as an autonomous intellectual realm." p. 126. In his *theory of multiple intelligences*, Gardner gives these supporting arguments for identifying *musical intelligence* as a separate and unique intelligence: potential isolation by brain damage, the existence of savants and prodigies, an identifiable set of core operations, a distinctive developmental history, definable 'end-state' performances, an evolutionary history, support from experimental psychological tasks, support from psychometric findings, and susceptibility to encoding in a symbol system. p. 62-67.

stories of persons I have known: These are brief vignettes of meaningful moments I have known as a clinical music therapist. Personal identifiers have been removed in respect of confidentiality.

xviii. silences (p.58)

be a silent one: Max Picard; *The World of Silence.* "Speech came out of silence, out of the fullness of silence. The fullness of silence would have exploded if it had not been able to flow out into speech." p. 8. Gabriel Marcel notes in the Preface: "In Picard's volume, the reader will find a whole set of discussions on such topics as the relation of silence to love, to faith, to poetry — discussions which are each concrete approaches towards that reality which we today find it so difficult to reach." p. xiii.

silent one in solitude: Thomas Merton, Trappist monk; *Thomas Merton, Spiritual Master, the Essential Writings*: "When solitude was a problem, I had no solitude. When it ceased to be a problem, I found I already possessed it, and could have possessed it all along ... The solitary life, being silent, clears away the smoke-screen of words that man has laid down between his mind and things. In solitude we remain face to face with the naked being of things. And yet we find that the nakedness of reality which we have feared, is neither a matter of terror nor for shame. It is clothed in the friendly communion of silence, and this silence is related to love ... When we have lived long enough alone with the reality around us, our veneration will learn how to bring forth a few good words about it from the silence which is the mother of Truth." p. 244.

silent dream begins to sound in music: Renown Sufi musician, Hazrat Inayat Khan, describes in *The Mysticism Sound and Music* how his life became music: "I have found in every word a certain musical value, a melody in every thought, harmony in every feeling; and I have tried to interpret the same thing, with clear and simple words, to those who used to listen to my music. I played the vina until my heart turned into this very instrument; then I offered this instrument to the divine Musician, the only musician existing. Since then, I have become His flute; and when he chooses, He plays His music. The people give me credit for this music, which in reality is not due to me but to the Musician who plays on His own instrument." p. xvii. So, this musical being has transformed into a musical instrument of a higher cause.

silent pause between two sounded tones: Cognitively we measure the spaces between the pulses, and from accent to accent, to lock into the beat; music always born in silence for us.

Bibliography for Part One

Aigen, Kenneth. *Music-Centered Music Therapy*. Gilsum, NH: Barcelona, 2005.

Ball, Philip. *Music Instinct: How Music Works and Why We Can't Do without It*. Oxford: Oxford University Press, 2010.

Barnhart, Robert, ed. *Chambers Dictionary of Etymology*. London: Chambers Harrap, 2010. First published in 1988.

Bekoff, Marc. *The Emotional Lives of Animals*. Novata, California: New World Library, 2007.

Belkin, Alan. *Musical Composition: Craft and Art*. New Haven, CT: Yale University Press, 2018.

Bertalanffy, Ludwig von. *General System Theory: Foundations, Development, Applications*. Revised edition. New York: Braziller, 2009.

Bierhorst, John, ed. *The Red Swan: Myths and Tales of American Indians*. Farrar, Strauss and Giroux: New York, 1976.

Brown, Steven. "The 'Musilanguage' Model of Music Evolution." In *The Origins of Music*, 271–300. Edited by Nils L. Wallin, Bjorn Merker, and Steven Brown. Cambridge, MA: MIT Press, 2000.

Bruscia, Kenneth. *Defining Music Therapy*. 2nd ed. Gilsum, NH: Barcelona Publishers, 1998.

Buber, Martin. *I and Thou*. Translated by Kaufmann, Walter. New York: Simon & Schuster, 1996.

Budd, Malcolm. *Music and the Emotions: The Philosophical Theories*. International Library of Philosophy. London: Routledge & Kegan Paul, 1985.

Buzsáki, György. *Rhythms of the Brain*. Oxford: New York: Oxford University Press, 2006.

Campbell, Murray, and Clive Greated. *The Musicians' Guide to Acoustics*. New York: Schirmer Books, 1988.

Corkery, Daniel. *The Hidden Ireland: A Study of Gaelic Munster in the Eighteenth Century*. Dublin: Gill and Macmillan, 1967. Originally published in 1924.

Creese, David. *The Monochord in Ancient Greek Harmonic Science*. Cambridge: Cambridge University Press, 2010.

Coomaraswamy, Ananda. *The Dance of Shiva*. New Delhi: Rupa Publications, 2013.

Cross, Ian. "The Nature of Music and its Evolution." In the *The Oxford Handbook of Music Psychology*, 3-13. Edited by Susan Hallam, Ian Cross, and Michael Thaut. Oxford: Oxford University Press, 2008.

Curtis, Natalie. *The Indians Book*. New York: Harper and Brothers, 1907.

Davies, Stephen. *Philosophical Perspectives on Art*. Oxford: Oxford University Press, 2007.

Elkington, David. *The Ancient Language of Sacred Sound: The Acoustic Science of the Divine*. Rochester, VT: Inner Traditions, 2021.

Flanagan, Joseph. *Quest for Self-Knowledge.* Toronto: University of Toronto Press, 1997.

Foster, Russell, and Leon Kreitzman. *Rhythms of Life: The Biological Clocks That Control the Daily Lives of Every Living Thing.* London: Profile Books, 2004.

Fowke, Edith. *Chansons de Québec.* Waterloo, ON: Waterloo Music, 1958.

Fowke, Edith. *Folklore of Canada.* Toronto: McClelland & Stewart, 1976.

Gardner, Howard. *Frames of Mind: The Theory of Multiple Intelligences.* New York: Basic Books, 1993.

Gioia, Ted. *Work Songs.* Durham, NC: Duke University Press, 2006.

Gouk, Penelope, ed. *Musical Healing in Cultural Contexts.* Brookfield, VT: Ashgate, 2000.

Guthrie, W.K.C. *The Earlier Presocratics and the Pythagoreans: Vol. 1. A History of Greek Philosophy.* Cambridge: Cambridge University Press, 1962

Hallam, Susan, Ian Cross, and Michael Thaut, eds. *The Oxford Handbook of Music Psychology.* Oxford: Oxford University Press, 2009.

Hatcher, John. *The Face of God Among Us.* Wilmette, IL: Bahá'í Publishing, 2010.

Havens, Ronald. *The Wisdom of Milton H. Erickson.* Bethel, CT: Crown House, 2003.

Heller, Agnes. *A Theory of Feelings.* 2nd ed. New York: Lexington Books, 2009.

Hodges, Donald. *A Concise Survey of Music Philosophy.* New York: Routledge, 2017.

Horden, Peregrine, ed. *Music as Medicine: The History of Music Therapy since Antiquity.* Brookfield, VT: Ashgate, 2000.

Ihde, Don. *Listening and Voice: Phenomenologies of Sound.* 2nd ed. Albany, NY: State University of New York Press, 2007.

Janzen, Thenille B. and Michael H. Thaut. "Cerebral Organization of Music Processing." In *The Oxford Handbook of Music and the Brain*, 89-121. Edited by Michael H. Thaut and Donald A. Hodges. Oxford: Oxford University Press, 2019.

Jenny, Hans. *Cymatics: A Study of Wave Phenomena and Vibration.* Eliot, ME: MACROmedia Publishing, 1967, 1974.

Juslin, Patrik N., and John A. Sloboda, eds. *Music and Emotion: Theory and Research.* Oxford: Oxford University Press, 2001.

Kahn, Hazrat Inayat. *The Mysticism Sound and Music.* Boulder, CO: Shambhala Publications, Revised edition, 1996.

Kenny, Carolyn. *Listening, Playing, Creating: Essays on the Power of Sound.* Albany, NY: State University of New York Press, 1995.

Koen, Bernard, ed. *The Oxford Handbook of Medical Ethnomusicology.* Oxford: Oxford University Press, 2011.

Krause, Bernie. *The Great Animal Orchestra.* New York: Little, Brown and Company, 2012.

Krishnamurti, Jiddu. *On Relationship*. New York: HarperOne, 1992.

Kuntz, Paul. *Whitehead's Category of Harmony*. Process Studies 29 (1): 43-65 (2000), https://scholarlypublishingcollective.org/uip/ps/article-abstract/29/1/43/210479/Whitehead-s-Category-of-Harmony-Analogous-Meanings.

Langer, Susanne. *Philosophy in a New Key*. 3rd ed. Cambridge, MA: Harvard University Press, 1957.

Laszlo, Ervin. *Science and the Akashic Record*. 2nd ed. Rochester, VT: Inner Traditions, 2007.

Laszlo, Ervin. *The Systems View of the World: A Holistic Vision for Our Time*. Cresskill, NJ: Hampton Press, 1996.

Lauzon, Paul. "Close Encounters of the Musical Kind." In *Listening, Playing, Creating: Essays on the Power of Sound*, 128–36. Edited by Carolyn Kenny. Albany, NY: State University of New York Press, 1995.

Lauzon, Paul. 2006. "Change in Music Therapy: A Discourse". 33rd National Conference of the Canadian Association for Music Therapy in Windsor, ON, May 4–8, 2006.

Lauzon, Paul. 2011. "Anatomy of a Musical Being: A Music Systems Theory of Music Therapy". Voices: A World Forum for Music Therapy 11 (1). https://doi.org/10.15845/voices.v11i1.163.

Lauzon, Paul. (2017). "Folk song as a therapeutic resource." *Canadian Journal for Music Therapy*, 23, 59–77.

Lauzon, Paul Laurent. "Music and Spirituality: Explanations and Implications for Music Therapy." British Journal of Music Therapy 34, no. 1 (May 2020): 30–38. https://doi.org/10.1177/1359457520908263

Levarie, Siegmund, and Ernst Levy. *Tone: A Study in Musical Acoustics*. 2d ed. Westport, CT: Greenwood Press, 1981.

Levarie, Siegmund, and Ernst Levy. *Musical Morphology: A Discourse and a Dictionary*. Kent, OH: Kent State University Press, 1983.

Lomax, Alan. "Folk song style". In *Alan Lomax: Selected writings, 1934–1997*, 139–172. Edited by R. Cohen. New York: Routledge, 2003. Reprinted from American Anthropologist, vol. 61, no. 6, 927–954, 1959.

Lonergan, Bernard. "The Subject." In *Collected Works of Bernard Lonergan: A Second Collection*. 60-74. Edited by Robert Doran and John Dadosky. Toronto: University of Toronto Press, 2016.

Lonergan, Bernard. *Method in Theology*. Toronto: University of Toronto press, 1994.

Lonergan, Bernard. *Topics in Education*. Vol. 10 of *Collected Works*. Toronto: University of Toronto Press, 1993.

Lord, Albert B. *The Singer of Tales*. Harvard Studies in Comparative Literature 24. Cambridge, MA: Harvard University Press, 1981.

Lovelock, James. *Gaia: A New Look at Life on Earth*. Oxford: Oxford University Press, 2000. First published, 1979.

Mathieu, W. A. *Harmonic Experience*. Rochester, VT: Inner Traditions, 1997.

McGilchrist, Iain. *The Master and His Emissary: The Divided Brain and the Making of the Western World.* New Expanded Edition. New Haven, CT: Yale University Press, 2019. First published, 2009.

Merriam, Alan P. *The Anthropology of Music.* Evanston, IL: Northwestern University Press, 1987.

Merton, Thomas, and Lawrence Cunningham. *Thomas Merton, Spiritual Master: The Essential Writings.* New York: Paulist Press, 1992.

Mithen, Steven. *The Singing Neanderthals: The Origin of Music, Language, Mind and Body.* London: Phoenix, 2006.

New Jerusalem Bible: Standard Edition. New York: Doubleday, 1989.

Nordoff, Paul, Clive Robbins, and David Marcus. *Creative Music Therapy: A Guide to Fostering Clinical Musicianship.* 2nd edition, revised and expanded by Clive Robbins. Gilsum, NH: Barcelona, 2007.

Parncutt, Richard. "Prenatal development and the phylogeny and ontogeny of music." In the *The Oxford Handbook of Music Psychology*, 219-228. Edited by Susan Hallam, Ian Cross, and Michael Thaut. Oxford: Oxford University Press, 2009.

Patel, Aniruddh D. *Music, Language, and the Brain.* New York: Oxford University Press, 2008.

Payne, Roger. *Among Whales.* New York: Scribner, 1995.

Picard, Max. *The World of Silence.* Southport, UK: CC Publishing, 2023. First published in 1948.

Rahner, Karl. *The Need and the Blessing of Prayer.* Collegeville, MN: Liturgical Press, 1997.

Ravenscroft, Ian. *Philosophy of Mind.* Oxford: Oxford University Press, 2005

Rider, Mark. *The Rhythmic Language of Health and Disease.* Saint Louis, MO: MMB Music, 1997.

Rossi, Ernest Lawrence, and David Nimmons. *The 20-Minute Break: Reduce Stress, Maximize Performance, and Improve Health and Emotional Well-Being Using the New Science of Ultradian Rhythms.* New York: J.P. Tarcher. Distributed by St. Martin's Press, 1991.

Russon, John. *Bearing Witness to Epiphany: Persons, Things, and the Nature of Erotic Life.* SUNY Series in Contemporary Continental Philosophy. Albany, NY: SUNY Press, 2009.

Sachs, Curt. *The History of Musical Instruments.* New York: W.W. Norton & Company, 1940.

Small, Christopher. *Musicking: The Meanings of Performing and Listening.* Hanover, NH: University Press of New England, 1998.

Steffen, Patrick, Dawson Hedges and Rebekka Matheson. "The Brain is Adaptive Not Triune: How the Brain Responds to Threat, Challenge, and Change." *Frontiers of Psychiatry 13: 802606* (April 2022). doi:10:3389/fpsyt.2022.802606

Steiner, George. *Real Presences.* Chicago: University of Chicago Press, 1989.

Teilhard de Chardin, Pierre. *The Phenomenon of Man.* Translated by Bernard Wall. New York: Harper and Row, 1965. Originally published in 1955 by Editions du Seuil, Paris.

Thaut, Michael. *Rhythm, Music, and the Brain: Scientific Foundations and Clinical Applications.* Studies on New Music Research 7. New York: Routledge, 2005.

Thaut, Michael, and Donald A. Hodges, eds. *The Oxford Handbook of Music and the Brain.* Oxford: Oxford University Press, 2019.

Thompson, William Forde. *Music, Thought, and Feeling: Understanding the Psychology of Music.* Oxford: Oxford University Press, 2009.

Trehub, Sandra. "Music lessons from infants." In the *The Oxford Handbook of Music Psychology*, 229-234. Edited by Susan Hallam, Ian Cross, and Michael Thaut. Oxford: Oxford University Press, 2009.

Turner, Edith. *Communitas: The Anthropology of Collective Joy.* New York: Palgrave MacMillan, 2012.

Wallin, Nils Lennart, Björn Merker, and Steven Brown, eds. *The Origins of Music.* Cambridge, MA: MIT Press, 2000.

Watzlawick, Paul, John H. Weakland, and Richard Fisch. *Change: Principles of Problem Formation and Problem Resolution.* New York: W.W. Norton & Co, 2011.

Wheeler, Barbara L., ed. *Music Therapy Handbook.* New York: The Guilford Press, 2015.

Whitehead, Alfred North. *Adventures in Ideas.* New York: Free Press, 1967. Originally published in 1933.

Wolff, Christoph. *Johann Sebastian Bach: The Learned Musician.* New York: W.W. Norton, 2000.

Works Cited in Part Two

Aigen, K. *Music-Centered Music Therapy*. Gilsum, NH: Barcelona Publishers, 2005.

Aldridge, D., and Aldridge, G. "Life as Jazz: Hope, Meaning, and Music Therapy in the Treatment of Life-Threatening Illness." In Dileo, C. (Ed.), 1999. *Music Therapy and Medicine* (pp. 79–94). Silver Spring, MD: American Music Therapy Association, 1999.

Aldridge, D. *From out of the Silence: Music Therapy Research and Practice in Medicine*. London: Jessica Kingsley Publishers, 1996.

Audi, R. (Ed.). *The Cambridge Dictionary of Philosophy* (2nd ed.). Cambridge: Cambridge University Press, 1999.

Austin, D. *The Theory and Practice of Vocal Psychotherapy*. London: Jessica Kingsley Publishers, 2008.

Block, N., Flanagan, O., and Guzeldere, G. *The Nature of Consciousness*. Cambridge, MA: MIT Press, 1997.

Bonny, H. and Summer, L. *Music consciousness: The Evolution of Guided Imagery and Music*. Gilsum, NH: Barcelona Publishers, 2002.

Brown, S. The "Musilanguage" Model of Music. In Wallin, N.L., Merker, B., & Brown, S. (Eds.), *The Origins of Music* (pp. 271-300). Cambridge, MA: MIT Press, 2000.

Bruscia, K. *Improvisational Models of Music Therapy.* Springfield, IL: Charles C. Thomas, 1987.

Burrows, D. *Sound, Speech, and Music.* Amherst, MA: University of Massachusetts Press, 1990.

Davidson, M. *Uncommon Sense.* Los Angeles: J.P. Tarcher, 1983.

Eagle, C. "An Introductory Perspective on Music Psychology." In Hodges, D. (Ed). *Handbook of Music Psychology.* (2nd. ed.) (pp. 1–28) San Antonio, TX: IMR Press, 1996.

Gardner, H. *Frames of Mind.* New York: Basic Books, 1993.

Guthrie, W.K.C. *The Earlier Presocratics and the Pythagoreans: Vol. 1. A History of Greek Philosophy.* Cambridge: Cambridge University Press, 1962.

Hodges, D. (Ed). *Handbook of Music Psychology.* (2nd ed.). San Antonio, TX: IMR Press, 1996.

Honderich, T. *Philosopher: A Kind of Life.* London: Routledge, 2001.

Kenny, C. *Music and Life in the Field of Play: An Anthology.* Gilsum, NH: Barcelona Publishers, 2006.

Langer, S. *Philosophy in a New Key.* (3rd Ed.). Cambridge, MA: Harvard University Press, 1957.

Laszlo, E. *A Systems View of the World.* New York: George Braziller, 1996.

Laszlo, E. *Introduction to Systems Philosophy.* New York: Gordon and Breach, 1972.

Lauzon, P. Change in Music Therapy: A Discourse. *Proceedings of the National Conference, Canadian Association for Music Therapy* (pp. 2-17), 2006.

Lauzon, P. "The Playwheel: A model for therapeutic improvisation." *Canadian Journal of Music Therapy*, Vol. XII, no. 1, 92-107, 2006.

Leonard, G. *The Silent Pulse*. New York: New American Library, 1978.

Levarie, S. and Levy, E. *Musical Morphology: A Discourse and a Dictionary*. Kent, OH: Kent State University Press, 1983.

Levitin, D. *This is Your Brain on Music*. New York: Dutton, 2006.

Marcel, G. *The Mystery of Being (Volume II: Faith and Reality)*. Trans. by G.S. Fraser. South Bend, IN: St. Augustine's Press, 2001.

Nordoff, P. and Robbins, C. *Creative Music Therapy* (Rev. ed.). Gilsum, NH: Barcelona Publishers, 2007.

Oxford English Reference Dictionary, 2nd Edition, London: Oxford University Press, 1996.

Patel, A. *Music, Language, and the Brain*. Oxford: Oxford University Press, 2008.

Pavlicevic, M. *Music Therapy in Context*. London: Jessica Kingsley Publishers, 1997.

Pivcevic, E. *Change and Selves*. Oxford: Clarendon Press, 1990.

Priestley, M. *Essays on Analytical Music Therapy*. Gilsum, NH: Barcelona Publishers, 1994.

Ravenscroft, I. *Philosophy of Mind*. Oxford: Oxford University Press, 2005.

Read, H. *The Meaning of Art*. London: Faber Paperbacks, 1990.

Rider, M. *The Rhythmic Language of Health and Disease*. Saint Louis, MO: MMB Music, 1997.

Roget, P.M. *Roget's International Thesaurus*. Toronto: Fitzhenry and Whiteside, 1977.

Ruud, E. *Improvisation, Communication, and Culture*. Gilsum, NH: Barcelona Publishers, 1998.

Ruud, E. *Music Therapy and Its Relationship to Current Treatment Theories*. St. Louis: MO: MMB Music, 1978.

Sacks, O. *Musicophilia: Tales of Music and the Brain*. New York: Knopf, 2007.

Schneck, D. and Berger, D. *The Music Effect*. London: Jessica Kingsley Publishers, 2006.

Skyttner, L. *General Systems Theory: Ideas and Applications*. London: World Scientific Publishing, 2001.

Smeijsters, H. *Sounding the Self: Analogy in Improvisational Music Therapy*. Gilsum, NH: Barcelona Publishers, 2005.

Stige, B. *Culture-centered music therapy*. Gilsum, NH: Barcelona Publishers, 2002.

Taylor, D. *Biomedical Foundations of Music as Therapy*. Saint Louis, MO: MMB Music, 1997.

Thaut, M., Davis, W., and Gfeller, K. *An Introduction to Music Therapy: Theory and Practice.* (2nd Ed.). New York: McGraw-Hill, 1999.

Tillich, P. *Systematic Theology (Three volumes in one).* Chicago: University of Chicago Press, 1967.

Von Bertalanffy, L. *General System Theory.* New York: George Braziller, 1968.

Von Bertalanffy, L. *Problems of Life.* New York: Harper & Brothers, 1960.

Wigram, T., Pederson, I., and Bonde, L. *A Comprehensive Guide to Music Therapy.* London: Jessica Kingsley Publishers, 2002.

Winnicott, D.W. *Playing and Reality.* London: Routledge, 2005.

Works Consulted for Part Two

Barrow, J.D. *New Theories of Everything*. Oxford: Oxford University Press, 2007.

Blacking, J. *How Musical is Man*. Seattle, WA: University of Washington Press, 1974.

Bruscia, K. *Defining Music Therapy*. 2d ed. Gilsum, NH: Barcelona Publishers, 1998.

Bruscia, K. (Ed.) *The Dynamics of Music Psychotherapy*. Gilsum, NH: Barcelona Publishers, 1998.

Capra, F. and Luisi, P.L. *The Systems View of Life: A Unifying Vision*. New York: Cambridge University Press, 2014.

Capra, F. *The Web of Life: A New Scientic Understanding of Living Systems*. New York: Anchor Books, 1996.

Hallam, S., Cross, I., and Thaut, M. *The Oxford Handbook of Music Psychology*, Oxford: Oxford University Press, 2009..

Lauzon, P. *Materia Musica: A Philosophy of Music Therapy*. Unpublished master's thesis, Dallas, TX: Southern Methodist University, 1992.

Nordoff, P. and Robbins, C. *Therapy in Music for Handicapped Children*. London: Victor Gollancz, 1971.

Rossi, E. *The 20 Minute Break*. Los Angeles: J. P. Tarcher, 1991.

Rossi, E. *The Psychobiology of Mind-Body Healing*. New York: W.W. Norton, 1986.

Thompson, W.F. *Music, Thought, and Feeling*. Oxford: Oxford University Press, 2009.

Von Bertalanffy, L. *Robots, Men and Minds*. New York: George Braziller, 1967.

Acknowledgements

It takes a village to raise a child, a global village of mind and heart to make a book. I thank my partner Rosemary MacPhee, the first person to hear and appreciate these poems. I've shared the joy of making music with long time musical friends Ron Taddeo, Reg Savage, Ron Johnson, Bill Lauf, Rick Whitelaw, Chris Rawlings, Richard Gibson, Steven Peacock, and Kevin Herring. Authors I have known—Wendy Dathan, Peter Cunningham, Suzanne Schuurman, Michel Laverdière, and Alden Nowlan—have listened on the way. I thank my profoundest influence in music therapy, the late Fran Herman. My dear sisters Christine, Marie, Jocelyne, and Jeannie have been ever encouraging....

I thank Keith Helmuth for his enthusiasm as reader and editor of this work. I appreciate the family that is Chapel Street Editions—Keith, Ellen, and Brendan.

About the Author

Paul Lauzon is a poet, songwriter, and music therapist. For decades, his work has focused on exploring the many interconnections of sound and sense, of music and words. As a singer/songwriter, he has toured widely and released several recordings of original songs. As a clinical music therapist, he has worked with individuals in stages of life from pre-natal to palliative care. His peer-reviewed articles have appeared in several international music therapy journals. He is founding professor of the Music Therapy Program at Acadia University in Wolfville, Nova Scotia.

This is his first published book of poems. Working with Chapel Street Editions has drawn him back to his roots along the Wolastoq (Saint John River) in New Brunswick.